ROMANS

Who We Really Are

Romans 1–7

Group Directory

Pass this Directory around and have your Group Members
fill in their names and phone numbers

Name	Phone

ROMANS

Who We Really Are

Romans 1–7

EDITING AND PRODUCTION TEAM:
James F. Couch, Jr., Lyman Coleman, Sharon Penington,
Cathy Tardif, Christopher Werner, Matthew Lockhart,
Erika Tiepel, Richard Peace, Andrew Sloan,
Mike Shepherd, Katharine Harris, Scott Lee

NASHVILLE, TENNESSEE

Published by Serendipity House Publishers
Nashville, Tennessee

International Standard Book Number: 1-57494-319-7

ACKNOWLEDGMENTS

Scripture quotations are taken from the Holman Christian Standard Bible,
© Copyright 2000 by Holman Bible Publishers. Used by permission.

Nashville, Tennessee
1-800-525-9563
www.serendipityhouse.com

Table of Contents

Core Values

Community: The purpose of this curriculum is to build community within the body of believers around Jesus Christ.

Group Process: To build community, the curriculum must be designed to take a group through a step-by-step process of sharing your story with one another.

Interactive Bible Study: To share your "story," the approach to Scripture in the curriculum needs to be open-ended and right brain—to "level the playing field" and encourage everyone to share.

Developmental Stages: To provide a healthy program throughout the four stages of the life cycle of a group, the curriculum needs to offer courses on three levels of commitment: (1) Beginner Level—low-level entry, high structure, to level the playing field; (2) Growth Level—deeper Bible study, flexible structure, to encourage group accountability; (3) Discipleship Level—in-depth Bible study, open structure, to move the group into high gear.

Target Audiences: To build community throughout the culture of the church, the curriculum needs to be flexible, adaptable and transferable into the structure of the average church.

Mission: To expand the Kingdom of God one person at a time by filling the "empty chair." (We add an extra chair to each group session to remind us of our mission.)

Introduction

Each healthy small group will move through various stages as it matures.

Growth Stage: Here the group begins to care for one another as it learns to apply what they learn through Bible study, worship and prayer.

Develop Stage: The inductive Bible study deepens while the group members discover and develop gifts and skills. The group explores ways to invite their neighbors and coworkers to group meetings.

Birth Stage: This is the time in which group members form relationships and begin to develop community. The group will spend more time in ice-breaker exercises, relational Bible study and covenant building.

Multiply Stage: The group begins the multiplication process. Members pray about their involvement in new groups. The "new" groups begin the life cycle again with the Birth Stage.

Subgrouping: If you have nine or more people at a meeting, Serendipity recommends you divide into subgroups of 3–6 for the Bible study. Ask one person to be the leader of each subgroup and to follow the directions for the Bible study. After 30 minutes, the Group Leader will call "time" and ask all subgroups to come together for the Caring Time.

Each group meeting should include all parts of the "three-part agenda."

Ice-Breaker: Fun, history-giving questions are designed to warm the group and to build understanding about the other group members. You can choose to use all of the Ice-Breaker questions, especially if there is a new group member that will need help in feeling comfortable with the group.

Bible Study: The heart of each meeting is the reading and examination of the Bible. The questions are open, discover questions that lead to further inquiry. Reference notes are provided to give everyone a "level playing field." The emphasis is on understanding what the Bible says and applying the truth to real life. The questions for each session build. There is always at least one "going deeper" question provided. You should always leave time for the last of the "questions for interaction." Should you choose, you can use the optional "going deeper" question to satisfy the desire for the challenging questions in groups that have been together for a while.

Caring Time: All study should point us to actions. Each session ends with prayer and direction in caring for the needs of the group members. You can choose between several questions. You should always pray for the "empty chair." Who do you know that could fill that void in your group?

Sharing Your Story: These sessions are designed for members to share a little of their personal lives each time. Through a number of special techniques each member is encouraged to move from low risk, less personal sharing to higher risk responses. This helps develop the sense of community and facilitates caregiving.

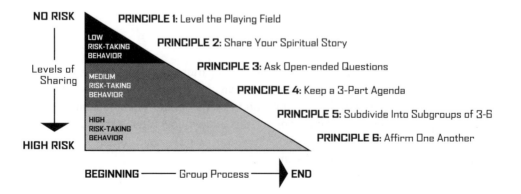

Group Covenant: A group covenant is a "contract" that spells out your expectations and the ground rules for your group. It's very important that your group discuss these issues—preferably as part of the first session.

GROUND RULES:

- Priority: While you are in the group, you give the group meeting priority.

- Participation: Everyone participates and no one dominates.

- Respect: Everyone is given the right to their own opinion and all questions are encouraged and respected.

- Confidentiality: Anything that is said in the meeting is never repeated outside the meeting.

- Empty Chair: The group stays open to new people at every meeting.

- Support: Permission is given to call upon each other in time of need—even in the middle of the night.

- Advice Giving: Unsolicited advice is not allowed.

- Mission: We agree to do everything in our power to start a new group as our mission.

ISSUES:

- The time and place this group is going to meet is_____

- Refreshments are _____ responsibility.

- Child care is _____ responsibility.

Greetings From Paul

Scripture Romans 1:1–7

After Jerusalem, he planned to travel to Spain, stopping en route to fulfill a long-held dream. He would visit Rome—the capital of the world. In anticipation of that visit, he wrote the letter to the Romans by way of introduction (the Roman Christians did not know him, though as Chapter 16 reveals, he had friends there). He was also eager to assure the Roman Christians, contrary to false rumors they might have heard, that the Gospel he was preaching was, indeed, the Gospel of Jesus Christ. Paul wrote his letter during a three-month period spent in Corinth at the home of his friend and convert Gaius (16:23). The time was probably A.D. 56–57, toward the end of his third missionary journey.

Paul's plan did not work as he intended. He would visit Rome, but not for three more years, and then he would come not as a tourist but as a prisoner. His misgivings about his Jerusalem trip proved accurate. Once there, he was quickly arrested and eventually sent to Rome for trial. Paul remained in Rome under house arrest for at least two years. Ultimately, according to reliable tradition, he was executed at a place just outside Rome. He never went to Spain.

It is not known how the Roman church began. Possibly some Roman Jews who were converted on the Day of Pentecost (Acts 2:10), began the church. As for the Gentile Christians in Rome, it is known that other Christian missionaries besides Paul were active in founding churches.

The book of Romans is Paul's most complete and carefully written theological statement. It is alive and vibrant, colorful, compassionate and sweeping in scope. The main issue Paul is addressing is the question of how God will judge each of us on the final day. Will it be on the basis of how "good" we were; that is, how well we kept the Law? If so, our lives would be full of unending tension. Acutely aware of repeated failure, we would never have any assurance of acquittal. The Law would then be a

Welcome to this study of Romans! Together we will engage in a study of one of the most foundational books of the Bible as we learn about the core doctrines of the Christian faith. For nearly 10 years Paul had been evangelizing the Gentile territories around the Aegean Sea. Now he turns his eyes to fresh fields. He wanted to go to Spain, the oldest Roman colony in the West. But first, with some misgivings (15:31), Paul is about to return to Jerusalem with a collection from the newer churches for the believers in Jerusalem.

cursed thing to us—a constant reminder of our inadequacy. But this is not how God intends life to be. Here the great theme of Romans emerges: We can have assurance of right standing before God and hence know we will be given a positive verdict on Judgment Day. Such confidence does not come because of what we have done. It comes because God, through Christ's death in our place, freely offers us his grace. Salvation is a gift that we cannot earn; we can only receive it by faith with such gratitude that our whole life changes.

Paul sets this theme against the teaching of certain Jewish Christians, legalists who would add circumcision to grace (thus nullifying grace). If we have to do anything to deserve it, salvation is not an unearned gift freely given by God. In the course of his argument, Paul sets up a series of opposites: faith versus works, Spirit versus flesh, and liberty versus bondage.

In answering the question of how people gain right standing before God, Paul argues first that both Gentile and Jew stand condemned before God (1:18–3:20); that it is only by God's grace shown in Christ's sacrificial death and accepted by faith that such right standing is found (3:21–5:23); and that such righteousness leads to a whole new lifestyle (6:1–8:39). He then deals with the question of why Israel rejected Christ (9:1–11:36), ending with practical exhortations for a life of faith (12:1–15:13).

Ice-Breaker Connect With Your Group (15 minutes)

Today we are beginning a study of one of the most important books of the New Testament–Romans. We begin with a look at the author of this book and his self-introduction. Take some time and introduce yourselves to one another by sharing your responses to the following questions.

Leader
Be sure to read the introductory material in the front of this book prior to this first session. To help your group members get acquainted, have each person introduce him or herself and then take turns answering one or two of the Ice-Breaker questions. If time allows, you may want to discuss all three questions.

1. If you were to write your own biography, what would be the title of the book?

   ○ I Did It My Way.
   ○ Faith, Hope and Love.
   ○ Living on the Edge.
   ○ Life Happened.
   ○ Life of the Party.
   ○ Other _____.

2. What part of your family heritage do you want to see passed on to relatives who follow you?

3. If you were to go on a trip knowing that it might be your last, where would you want to be traveling?

📖 Bible Study   Read Scripture and Discuss (30 minutes)

Credibility is critical when delivering an important message. This is especially true if you have some past life experiences that are public and may cause doubt in those you are trying to reach. Paul begins by establishing his credibility as an apostle and reminds his readers of the mission of all of those who follow Christ. Read Romans 1:1–7 and note how Paul describes himself.

Leader
Select a member of the group ahead of time to read aloud the Scripture passage. Then discuss the Questions for Interaction, dividing into subgroups of three to six. Be sure to save time at the end for the Caring Time.

Greetings From Paul

1 Paul, a slave of Christ Jesus, called as an apostle and singled out for God's good news—²which He promised long ago through His prophets in the Holy Scriptures—³concerning His Son, Jesus Christ our Lord, who was a descendant of David according to the flesh ⁴and was established as the powerful Son of God by the resurrection from the dead according to the Spirit of holiness. ⁵We have received grace and apostleship through Him to bring about the obedience of faith among all the nations, on behalf of His name, ⁶including yourselves who are also Jesus Christ's by calling:

⁷To all who are in Rome, loved by God, called as saints.

⁸Grace to you and peace from God our Father and the Lord Jesus Christ.

Romans 1:1–7

Questions for Interaction

Leader
Refer to the Summary and Study Notes at the end of this session as needed. If 30 minutes is not enough time to answer all of the questions in this section, conclude the Bible Study by answering questions 6 and 7.

1. What three descriptive words would you use to introduce yourself to the group?

   ○ Accepting.
   ○ Courageous.
   ○ Fragile.
   ○ Imaginative.
   ○ Mischievous.
   ○ Predictable.
   ○ Sensitive.
   ○ Stubborn.
   ○ Other _____.

2. In introducing himself to the Christians in Rome, how does Paul describe himself? What truths about Jesus Christ does Paul proclaim in this passage?

3. What is Paul's mission in life? Who is he trying to reach with the Good News?

4. What does receiving "grace and apostleship through Him" (v. 5) mean to you?

5. How are we "called as saints" (v. 7)? What does it mean to be a saint?

6. Where are you in the journey of following Christ?

   ○ I've got lots of questions.
   ○ I'm just getting started.
   ○ I've been a follower for a couple of years.
   ○ I've been a follower my whole life.
   ○ I'm a mentor to new followers.
   ○ Other _____.

7. Who do you know that needs to receive the gift of God's saving grace? How can God use you to be a bridge of his grace to him or her?

Going Deeper   If your group has time and/or wants a challenge, go on to this question.

8. What role did the Holy Sprit play in declaring Jesus as the Son of God (v. 4b)? How does the Holy Spirit help us live a life that reflects Jesus Christ as Lord (8:10–11)?

Caring Time Apply the Lesson and Pray for One Another (15 minutes)

This very important time is for developing and expressing your concern for each other as group members by praying for one another.

1. Agree on the group covenant and ground rules (see the front of this book).

2. Pray for the people whose names were shared during question #7. Who else would you like to add to that list?

3. Share any other prayer requests and praises, and then close in prayer. Pray specifically for God to lead you to someone to bring next week to fill the empty chair.

Leader
Take some extra time in this first session to go over the introductory material at the beginning of this book. At the close, pass around your books and have everyone sign the Group Directory in the front of this book.

NEXT WEEK *Today we looked at the apostle Paul's calling by God to share the Good News with Gentiles. We saw that the basis for the apostleship gift given to Paul was the receiving of God's amazing grace, which he still freely gives to all people who will receive it. We were reminded of our responsibility as followers of Christ to share that grace and Good News with people in our lives. In the coming week, continue to pray for the person you mentioned in question #7. Ask the Holy Spirit to open his or her heart to receive God's grace. Next week we will look at Paul's prayer for and desire to visit the believers in Rome.*

Notes on Romans 1:1–7

Summary: Paul's life had been dramatically changed by the acceptance of God's grace. In his former life, he was known as a murderer of Christians. In his new life, his mission was to add more Christians to the kingdom of God. God had gifted him and made it clear what he was to do with his life. All followers of Christ should be reminded of the awesomeness of the grace we have received and of our obligation as recipients to share that grace with people God puts in our lives.

1:1 *Paul.* In introducing himself, Paul uses his Roman name and not his Jewish one (Saul). *slave.* A Greek did not think of himself as a slave of his king, though a Jew did—knowing that the king in turn counted himself a "slave of God." Old Testament prophets and leaders were called servants of God (Josh. 1:2). Paul is the willing servant of Jesus whom he identifies as "Lord" (v. 3); a Master in authority over such slaves. *called.* Paul did not just decide one day that he would like to be an apostle and thus declare himself such. He is an apostle because God appointed him to be one. *apostle.* In the broad sense, an apostle is anyone sent on a mission with a message. *singled out.* In two other places, the same word is used of Paul. In Galatians 1:15, God singles him out from birth for a special task, and in Acts 13:2 the church singles him out for a special mission. As a former Pharisee (Phil. 3:5), he once claimed to be set apart from other people to serve God, but now he finds that he has been set apart by God to serve people. *good news.* The message of the early church about Jesus Christ, focusing especially on his death and resurrection; a term whose Old Testament roots carries the idea of God's deliverance of his people from exile (Isa. 52:7–10), which is a foreshadowing of the New Testament idea of deliverance from the bondage of sin.

1:2 *promised long ago.* Having defined the Gospel as being "of God" in verse 1, Paul further specifies that the Gospel was a fulfillment of prophecy. It had been foretold by God's own prophets and recorded in sacred Scripture. Thus it is not surprising that within Romans Paul will prove various points about Jesus by reference back to the Old Testament Scriptures, where God first revealed his will and plans. Paul says all this about the Gospel so as to underline its complete trustworthiness. The Gospel is true because it is from God.

1:3–4 A short, creedal statement probably familiar to the Roman Christians (4:24–25; 10:8–10; and 16:25–26). This one is remarkably similar in structure to Peter's Pentecost sermon (Acts 2:22–28); i.e., Paul is preaching the apostolic Gospel.

1:4 *Son of God.* Jesus belongs to two spheres of existence: the human, in which he is the descendant of King David (from whose line the Messiah was to come); and the divine, in which he is God's Son (this fact having been verified through his resurrection). *Spirit of holiness.* This declaration was made through (literally, "in accord with") the Holy Spirit.

1:5 *grace and apostleship.* Paul did not earn the right or deserve to be an apostle. He is one because of God's "undeserved favor" ("grace"). *obedience of faith.* New Testament faith is not just intellectual belief that something is true, nor is it merely an emotional feeling of trust. It is active response to God—faith that shows itself in obedience (Gal. 5:6–8). *all the nations.* Paul's apostolic commission is quite specific. His ministry is to evangelize the non-Jewish world. There were others who were called to reach Jews (Gal. 2:7–10). Nevertheless, it is also true that Paul had a deep love and concern for his Jewish kinfolk (11:13–14).

Paul's Prayer and Desire to Visit Rome

Scripture Romans 1:8–17

LAST WEEK *In the last session, we looked at the apostle Paul's calling by God to share the Good News with Gentiles. We saw that the basis for the apostleship gift given to Paul was God's amazing grace, which he gives to all people who will receive it. In today's lesson, we will look at Paul's prayer for the believers in Rome and his desire to visit them. By Paul's example we will learn how we can best encourage each other in this group.*

Ice-Breaker Connect With Your Group (15 minutes)

Today we continue with Paul's opening remarks to the believers in Rome. He writes passionately about the people he longs to be with and about the saving faith that is ours through Christ Jesus. Take a moment and get to know one another by sharing your responses to the following questions.

Leader
Begin the session with a word of prayer. Have your group members take turns sharing their responses to one, two or all three of the Ice-Breaker questions. Be sure that everyone gets a chance to participate.

1. What is your most prized possession?

   ○ Money.
   ○ Jewelry.
   ○ Automobile.
   ○ Memento.
   ○ Family heirloom.
   ○ Other _____.

2. What is the greatest gift you have received in your life?

3. Who is someone you haven't seen for a long time and would love to see again?

⊟ Bible Study Read Scripture and Discuss (30 minutes)

Leader
Select a member of the group ahead of time to read aloud the Scripture passage. Then divide into subgroups of three to six and discuss the Questions for Interaction.

Paul begins with an expression of thankfulness and writes about the value of community. He then moves to the central message of this letter, the role of faith in salvation. Read Romans 1:8–17 and note the love Paul has for his brothers and sisters in Christ.

Paul's Prayer and Desire to Visit Rome

[8]First, I thank my God through Jesus Christ for all of you because the news of your faith is being reported in all the world. [9]For God, whom I serve with my spirit in telling the good news about His Son, is my witness that I constantly mention you, [10]always asking in my prayers that if it is somehow in God's will, I may now at last succeed in coming to you. [11]For I want very much to see you, that I may impart to you some spiritual gift to strengthen you, [12]that is, to be mutually encouraged by each other's faith, both yours and mine.

[13]Now I want you to know, brothers, that I often planned to come to you (but was prevented until now) in order that I might have a fruitful ministry among you, just as among the rest of the Gentiles. [14]I am obligated both to Greeks and barbarians, both to the wise and the foolish. [15]So I am eager to preach the good news to you also who are in Rome.

[16]For I am not ashamed of the gospel, because it is God's power for salvation to everyone who believes, first to the Jew, and also to the Greek. [17]For in it God's righteousness is revealed from faith to faith, just as it is written: The righteous will live by faith.

Romans 1:8–17

Questions for Interaction

Leader
Refer to the Summary and Study Notes at the end of this session as needed. If 30 minutes is not enough time to answer all of the questions in this section, conclude the Bible Study by answering questions 6 and 7.

1. Who are the people in your life that you are grateful for? Why?

2. Why was Paul thankful for the believers in Rome? What would Paul say about your small group?

3. Who has been a great encourager to you in your journey of following Christ?

4. What did Paul do to strengthen and encourage the faith of the believers in Rome? How did this also encourage him? Who in your group needs some encouragement today?

5. Paul felt obligated to preach the Good News to everyone, regardless of race or creed (v. 14). What do you feel is the biggest "obligation" in your life right now?

- ○ Mortgage.
- ○ Debt.
- ○ Retirement.
- ○ Career.
- ○ Family.
- ○ Neighbors.
- ○ God.
- ○ Other _____.

6. What do you need to change in order to be more "obligated" to God and his will for your life?

7. Paul was bold about his faith and "not ashamed of the gospel" (v. 16). When have you been in a situation where you felt like you "stuck out" in sharing your faith? Were you bold or embarrassed?

Going Deeper   If your group has time and/or wants a challenge, go on to this question.

8. Why do people try to gain salvation through their own merit, rather than accept God's righteousness through Jesus Christ? How strong a role does guilt play in this?

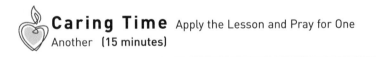 **Caring Time** Apply the Lesson and Pray for One Another (15 minutes)

Take some time now to be "mutually encouraged by each other's faith" (v. 12). Share your responses to the following questions and then support one another in prayer.

Leader
Bring the group back together and begin the Caring Time by sharing responses to all three questions. Then take turns sharing prayer requests and having a time of group prayer.

1. What spiritual gift would you like to develop that would strengthen your fellow believers?

2. Recall the ideas of encouragement shared from question 4. What can you do to encourage someone in the coming week?

3. What is your biggest concern about the coming week? In what way do you need to "live by faith" (v. 17)?

P.S. Add new group members to the Group Directory at the front of this book.

NEXT WEEK *Today we were reminded about how important community is to the Christian faith. Paul had an eagerness to connect at a deep level with people he didn't even know. We also examined how our salvation is totally dependent upon God. We only need to be open to and receive God's free gift. In the coming week, write a note of thanks and encouragement to your pastor or the person you mentioned in question #3 under the Questions for Interaction. Next week we will look at God's anger against the sin of humanity.*

Notes on Romans 1:8–17

Summary: In customary fashion, Paul moves from greeting to thanksgiving. He prays for the Roman Christians, announces his plans to visit, and defines what his letter is all about. The way of getting right with God has been provided by God himself and comes through faith alone in Jesus Christ.

1:8 *thank.* When Greeks wrote letters, immediately after the salutation they generally informed the recipients that they had offered a prayer to the gods on their behalf, often asking that they be given prosperity and good health. Once again, Paul seems to follow this convention (though not in a traditional fashion). *faith.* The stress is on the quality of their faith (it had been demonstrated by their lifestyle), not on the fact they believed in Jesus. *reported in all the world.* Paul had given similar praise to the Thessalonians (1 Thess. 1:7–8), so this is not just flattery reserved for those who live in the most important city.

1:12 *mutually encouraged.* Paul's attitude toward the Roman church is one of genuine humility and not one of arrogance because he is an apostle; he will need spiritual refreshment from them as well when he stops there en route to Spain.

1:14 *obligated.* This obligation stems from the fact that God has commissioned Paul to this ministry. *Greeks and barbarians.* This distinction is cultural and not racial or national. Even though Paul is writing to Romans, the Romans considered themselves culturally to be Greeks—a designation used as a synonym for the "wise" or "educated" (as against the "foolish" or "uneducated").

1:15 *eager.* Although "obligated" as an apostle, Paul discharges this task with joy and vigor.

1:16–17 Here Paul defines the central theme of Romans: The way of getting right with God has been provided by God himself and comes through faith alone. The rest of the epistle is an exposition of this point.

1:16 *salvation.* This word carries the Hebrew idea of salvation as wholeness and healing (in the here and now) as well as the idea of spiritual rescue (which will be realized in the future). *everyone who believes.* The required response to the message of salvation is faith; i.e., faith in the one about whom the message speaks: Jesus Christ. It is this response that culminates in salvation. *Jew ... Greek.* Another contrast which demonstrates the universality of Christianity.

1:17 *God'srighteousness.* In Hebrew thought, righteousness is not so much a moral quality as it is a legal judgment. The idea here is not that a person is made righteous (in the ethical sense) or proved righteous (virtuous) by such a pronouncement. Rather one is counted or reckoned as righteous, even though one is really guilty. Being thus pardoned, a person is given a right standing before God and can enter into a relationship with him. This declaration of righteousness comes from God to men and women—it is a reflection of God's character. He is righteous, and this fact shows itself in his saving activity. *from faith to faith.* What faith is becomes clear as the epistle unfolds, though in verse 5 its primary meaning has already been made clear—it is believing obedience. The one who has faith trusts that in the life, death and resurrection of Jesus Christ, one sees the power of God at work. He or she then responds to God by submitting to Jesus Christ and trusting solely in God's powerful work to save. *The righteous will live by faith.* This citation from Habakkuk 2:4 is the first of many quotes that Paul uses from the Old Testament to demonstrate and prove his point.

God's Anger at Sin

Scripture Romans 1:18–32

LAST WEEK *In the last session, we were reminded about how important community is to the Christian faith. We saw how Paul had an eagerness to connect at a deep level with people he didn't even know. We examined how our salvation is totally dependent upon God and that all we need to do is receive God's free gift. Today we will look at God's anger against the sin of humanity. We will be challenged with how we should respond to sin in our lives, within our group and with nonbelievers outside the church.*

 Ice-Breaker Connect With Your Group (15 minutes)

God teaches us through many situations. We can learn to appreciate his glory and creativity through the majesty of nature. We can also learn more of how he wants us to live through the tough love of discipline. Take turns sharing some teachable moments that you have experienced.

Leader
Choose one or two Ice-Breaker questions. If you have a new group member you may want to do all three. Remember to stick closely to the three-part agenda and the time allowed for each segment.

1. What experience causes you to stand in awe of God?

   ○ Being in the mountains.
   ○ Walking along the seashore.
   ○ Working in the garden.
   ○ Other _____.

2. As a child, what was the most usual method of discipline for bad behavior that you received?

3. What was your most embarrassing moment growing up?

   ○ Not getting to the restroom on time.
   ○ Receiving a traffic citation.
   ○ Hosting a wild party when my parents came home unexpectedly.
   ○ Getting caught without sufficient clothing.
   ○ Forgetting someone's birthday.
   ○ Other _____.

Bible Study Read Scripture and Discuss (30 minutes)

As we are about to read, God takes sin very seriously. It is why he had to send his only son Jesus to suffer and die. Sin is what destroys lives and communities and we must look at it from God's perspective. It makes his grace and forgiveness all the more meaningful. Read Romans 1:18–32 and note the consequences of sin.

Leader
Select a member of the group ahead of time to read aloud the Scripture passage. Then discuss the Questions for Interaction, dividing into subgroups of three to six.

God's Anger at Sin

[18]For God's wrath is revealed from heaven against all godlessness and unrighteousness of people who by their unrighteousness suppress the truth, [19]since what can be known about God is evident among them, because God has shown it to them. [20]From the creation of the world His invisible attributes, that is, His eternal power and divine nature, have been clearly seen, being understood through what He has made. As a result, people are without excuse. [21]For though they knew God, they did not glorify Him as God or show gratitude. Instead, their thinking became nonsense, and their senseless minds were darkened. [22]Claiming to be wise, they became fools [23]and exchanged the glory of the immortal God for images resembling mortal man, birds, four-footed animals, and reptiles.

[24]Therefore God delivered them over in the cravings of their hearts to sexual impurity, so that their bodies were degraded among themselves. [25]They exchanged the truth of God for a lie, and worshiped and served something created instead of the Creator, who is blessed forever. Amen.

[26]This is why God delivered them over to degrading passions. For even their females exchanged natural sexual intercourse for what is unnatural. [27]The males in the same way also left natural sexual intercourse with females and were inflamed in their lust for one another Males committed shameless acts with males and received in their own persons the appropriate penalty for their perversion.

[28]And because they did not think it worthwhile to have God in their knowledge, God delivered them over to a worthless mind to do what is morally wrong. [29]They are filled with all unrighteousness, evil, greed, and wickedness. They are full of envy, murder, disputes, deceit, and malice. They are gossips, [30]slanderers, God-haters, arrogant, proud, boastful, inventors of evil, disobedient to parents, [31]undiscerning, untrustworthy, unloving, and unmerciful. [32]Although they know full well God's just sentence—that those who practice such things deserve to die—they not only do them, but even applaud others who practice them.

Romans 1:18–32

Questions for Interaction

1. What are some things you have observed in nature that confirm to you the existence of God?

2. How does the reading of this passage make you feel?

3. In verses 21–23, what did people do to suppress the truth about God?

Leader
Refer to the Summary and Study Notes at the end of this session as needed. If 30 minutes is not enough time to answer all of the questions in this section, conclude the Bible Study by answering questions 6 and 7.

4. How did God respond to this failure to accept the truth? What does this say about how seriously God looks at sin in our lives?

5. Do you think our culture has changed much since this was written? Why or why not? How should we respond to people (believers and nonbelievers) who are struggling with sin?

6. What areas of temptation do you struggle with?

   ○ Money.
   ○ Sex.
   ○ Power.
   ○ Food.
   ○ Control.
   ○ Other _____.

7. How have you seen the consequences of sin affect your life? What have you learned from that experience?

Going Deeper   If your group has time and/or wants a challenge, go on to this question.

---

8. How should Christians view those who struggle with homosexuality? Why has the Christian church in general not been effective at reaching out to this group of people? What can we do to show our love for them despite our disagreement with this particular sin?

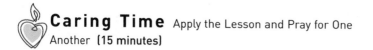

Caring Time
Apply the Lesson and Pray for One
Another (15 minutes)

Leader
Begin the Caring Time by having group members take turns sharing responses to all three questions. Be sure to save at least the last five minutes for a time of group prayer. Remember to include a prayer for the empty chair when concluding the prayer time.

Encouraging and supporting each other is especially vital if this group is to become all it can be. Take time now to share your struggles and pray for one another.

1. How is your relationship with Jesus right now?

   ○ Close.
   ○ Distant.
   ○ Improving.
   ○ Strained.
   ○ Other _____.

2. How can the group pray for you regarding the area(s) of temptation you shared in question #6?

3. What can you do in the coming week to counteract the influence of the secular culture on yourself and your family?

NEXT WEEK *Today we looked at God's anger against the sin of humanity. We were challenged with how we should respond to sin in our own lives, with people in our group and with nonbelievers. In the coming week, take time each evening to review your day and confess your sins. Next week we will look at how God judges humanity for sin, and how our response should be one of repentance and gratefulness for the kindness, restraint and patience of God.*

Summary: Paul's argument here is this: All people everywhere can know about God because the essential facts are written into nature itself. But knowing about God is not enough. Unless men and women honor him, their minds darken; they turn to various idolatries and become sinful beyond imagining.

In 1:19–20, Paul answers the unspoken objection: How can Gentiles be held accountable for their sins when they have never heard the truth? The failure of the Greek world was not that it denied God (atheism), but that it refused to worship and honor him. The issue is rebellion against God. The proper response to power and deity (v. 20) ought to be glorification and thankfulness (v. 21). In 1:24–28, God's wrath is being felt as he allows people to reap the inevitable fruit of their rebellion.

Not knowing (vv. 24–27) who their Creator is, their own identity becomes confused and is expressed in a distorted sexuality. Greek and Roman writers corroborate Paul's description: it was an age of unparalleled immorality. Paul selects a few representative examples from hundreds of possible Greek words that define specific forms of sin. This sin seeks to encourage others to join with itself in defiance of the awareness that ultimately there will be a judgment.

Paul reminds us of the seriousness of sin in our lives, within our communities and our world. We should be moved to reach out in love and make God's grace known to all people so they can be set free from the consequences of sin.

1:18 *God's wrath.* Because God is God and therefore holy and loving, he cannot tolerate evil, injustice, cruelty, etc. The Jews knew that on the coming Day of Judgment there must be punishment for sins (2:15–16). Such wrath is not irrational rage or anger, but rather the inevitable response of a good God to evil. ***revealed.*** Just as God's righteousness is being revealed (v. 17), so too is his wrath. Unless individuals see the reality of wrath, they may never see their need for being counted as righteous.

1:22 *fools.* In the Old Testament a fool was a person who lived with disregard to God.

1:23 *exchanged.* This word is used three times to indicate something of the nature of sin. It replaces God with idols, truth with lies (v. 25), and healthy relationships with harmful ones (v. 26). ***images.*** The center of life—that which claims first allegiance and guides choices—now shifts from God to "man" (family, tribe, leader, nation), to birds (e.g., the imperial Roman eagle), to animals (e.g., the golden calf in Exodus 32), and even to reptiles (worship of fear itself). All such idols will eventually prove unreliable, since they have no real power and will collapse under the weight of this wrongly directed worship.

1:24 *God delivered them over.* This phrase is also used three times (vv. 26,28) to indicate that God allowed people to carry out their rebellion and experience the fruit of their choices. ***sexual impurity.*** Defined by a Greek writer as "the passionate desire for forbidden pleasure."

1:29 *unrighteousness.* The opposite of justice: robbing God and others of their due. ***evil.*** The deliberate attempt to harm or to corrupt; such a person is not only intentionally bad, but seeks to make others so. ***greed.*** Taking whatever one wants without regard to the rights of others. ***wickedness.*** The most general term for badness; a vicious person devoid of any good quality. ***envy.*** Grudging resentment of (and desire for) another's accomplishments or possessions. ***murder.*** Jesus teaches that people must rid themselves of the very spirit of hatred, which issues in such a deed (Matt. 5:21–26). ***disputes.*** Contention born of envy. ***deceit.*** Underhanded, devious actions designed to get one's own way.

malice. Literally, "evil-nature"; always thinking the worst of another.

1:29–30 *gossips, slanderers.* The gossiper spreads ill news about others secretly, while the slanderer openly accuses.

1:30 *God-haters.* They hate God, because he is seen as inhibiting pleasure. *arrogant.* A sort of pride that arrogantly defies God and/or hurts and snubs others, simply for the delight in doing so. *boastful.* A word used for a medicine show quack who tries to impress others with his wares; a braggart. *inventors of evil.* Those who create new ways of sinning. *disobedient to parents.* For both Jews and Romans, obedience to parents was extremely important.

1:31 *undiscerning.* One who does not learn from experience. *untrustworthy.* One who breaks agreements. *unloving.* One without love for even family. *unmerciful.* One without pity who can harm or even kill without thought.

God Judges Sin

Scripture Romans 2:1–16

> **LAST WEEK** *In the last session, we looked at God's anger against the sin of humanity. We were challenged to look at the sin in our own lives and to evaluate our response to others who are struggling with sin. Today we will consider God's righteous judgment of sin and how none of us are innocent, though we tend to make judgments on other people. We will see how our response instead should be one of repentance and gratefulness for the kindness, restraint and patience of God.*

 **Ice-Breaker** Connect With Your Group (15 minutes)

Leader
Choose one, two or all three of the Ice-Breaker questions. Welcome and introduce new group members.

There is a certain fascination and interest when it comes to court cases and watching justice in action. We have all had experiences with the law, either on a personal level or just watching it in the media. Take turns sharing those experiences with one another.

1. What was your most recent experience with the police or other legal authority?

2. If you were to play a part in a high-profile court case, would you rather be the judge, a juror, the prosecutor, the defense attorney or an expert witness? Why?

3. Who do you think makes the best judge on TV?

   ○ Judge Judy.
   ○ Judge Joe Brown.
   ○ Judge Mills Lane.
   ○ Judge Jerry Sheindlin.
   ○ Judge Hatchett.

📖 Bible Study Read Scripture and Discuss (30 minutes)

People make judgments every day about how they are treated and how other people relate to them. Because God is righteous and holy he also judges our sin, with life-threatening consequences. Read Romans 2:1–16 and note the severity of God's judgment and the beauty of his grace.

Leader
Have a member of the group, selected ahead of time, read aloud the Scripture passage. Then discuss the Questions for Interaction, dividing into subgroups of three to six.

God Judges Sin

2 Therefore, anyone of you who judges is without excuse. For when you judge another, you condemn yourself, since you, the judge, do the same things. ²We know that God's judgment on those who do such things is based on the truth. ³Do you really think—anyone of you who judges those who do such things yet do the same—that you will escape God's judgment? ⁴Or do you despise the riches of His kindness, restraint, and patience, not recognizing that God's kindness is intended to lead you to repentance? ⁵But because of your hardness and unrepentant heart you are storing up wrath for yourself in the day of wrath, when God's righteous judgment is revealed. ⁶He will repay each one according to his works: ⁷eternal life to those who by patiently doing good seek for glory, honor, and immortality; ⁸but wrath and indignation to those who are self-seeking and disobey the truth, but are obeying unrighteousness; ⁹affliction and distress for every human being who does evil, first to the Jew, and also to the Greek; ¹⁰but glory, honor, and peace for everyone who does good, first to the Jew, and also to the Greek. ¹¹There is no favoritism with God.

¹²All those who sinned without the law will also perish without the law, and all those who sinned under the law will be judged by the law. ¹³For the hearers of the law are not righteous before God, but the doers of the law will be declared righteous. ¹⁴So, when Gentiles, who do not have the law, instinctively do what the law demands, they are a law to themselves even though they do not have the law. ¹⁵They show that the work of the law is written on their hearts. Their consciences testify in support of this, and their competing thoughts either accuse or excuse them ¹⁶on the day when God judges what people have kept secret, according to my gospel through Christ Jesus.

Romans 2:1–16

Questions for Interaction

Leader
Refer to the Summary and Study Notes at the end of this session as needed. If 30 minutes is not enough time to answer all of the questions in this section, conclude the Bible Study by answering questions 6 and 7.

1. What is something you get upset with others for that you are also guilty of?

   ○ Not using my turn signal.
   ○ Driving slowly in the left lane.
   ○ Leaving the "lid" up.
   ○ Talking during a movie.
   ○ Other _____ .

2. What does Paul say about those who are looking down on others?

3. How does God's kindness lead to repentance (v. 4)?

4. What are the consequences of not accepting God's kindness? What is meant by "storing up wrath for yourself" in verse 5 and "repay each one according to his works" in verse 6?

5. According to this text, none of us are innocent of sin no matter what our heritage may be. We are all guilty. Why do you think Christians tend to avoid "sinners" to the degree that we (generally speaking) have no unchurched friends? Why are we not effective at relating the Good News to those who do not commit the same "sins" as we do?

6. Where in your life do you need God to deal with your attitude toward people you tend to think are not as "good" as you are?

7. What does God's "kindness, restraint, and patience" mean to you personally when thinking of your own sin?

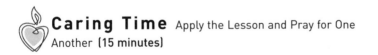

Going Deeper   If your group has time and/or wants a challenge, go on to this question.

8. How do you reconcile verse 7, "eternal life to those who by patiently doing good seek for glory, honor, and immortality;" with Paul's theme of Romans that we are justified by faith alone?

Caring Time   Apply the Lesson and Pray for One Another (15 minutes)

Take some time now to bring each other hope and support by sharing prayer requests and special concerns. Before closing in prayer, take turns sharing your answers to the following questions.

1. What is the worst thing that happened to you this last week? What was the best?

2. How are you doing at inviting others to our group?

3. How can the group pray for you regarding your answer to question #6?

Leader
Be sure to save the last 15 minutes for this important time. After sharing responses to all three questions and asking for prayer requests, close in a time of group prayer.

NEXT WEEK *Today we looked at how God is holy and righteous and therefore must judge the sin of humanity. We also considered how we judge others, even though none of us are innocent. We were reminded that instead of judging others, our response to God's grace should be one of repentance and gratefulness for his kindness, restraint and patience. In the coming week, pray for the people that you tend to judge. Next week we will see where the Jews got hung up on external measurements of spirituality and how we often do the same thing.*

Notes on Romans 2:1-16

Summary: Paul turns his focus from those who do evil and actually applaud its practice (Rom. 1:32) to those who do not applaud at all: the Jews and pagan moralists who consider themselves righteous because they are "above" the sins of others. Philosophers like Seneca and Marcus Aurelius would agree with Paul that the masses do, indeed, behave despicably. In like manner the Jews denounced pagan idolatry. But now Paul, like a prosecuting attorney, attacks this easy assumption of morality. He does so by adopting a style of composition common in those days—the diatribe. It is as if Paul picks out a member of the audience and gives him another point of view, which he (Paul) then attacks and refutes.

2:1–3 Paul argues that to agree that another person is guilty and deserving of judgment is to admit the existence of a law and a judge, and it is to accept the reality of judgment. Therefore, being a Jew or a philosopher does not save anyone, since they also from time to time do the very things God judges in Gentiles. To presume to judge another is to take upon oneself a role that belongs to God, and is therefore a form of idolatry!

2:4 Jews are presuming upon the mercy of God, taking his kindness as a sign of their immunity from judgment (when, in fact, such kindness was meant to lead them to change their lives, and not serve simply as an excuse for continued sinning). Jews would have looked forward to the day of God's wrath, believing that they would be vindicated while non-Jews would be punished. *kindness.* In Greek, there are two words for "goodness": one word refers to a sort of stern goodness that may issue in rebuke and punishment in the face of evil (e.g., Jesus with the money changers at the temple); the second word is the term used here: goodness with an air of kindliness about it (as with Jesus and the woman caught in adultery). *restraint.* Literally, a truce or a cessation of hostility. Paul's point is that this will not be unlimited. God's tolerance will end. *patience.* A word used of the person who has the power to gain revenge over another but chooses not to do so. So far God has been willing to endure their rejection. *repentance.* A change of mind about something that one has been doing that is wrong, coupled with the resolve to start doing the right thing. It is to such a change of heart that God's kindness, restraint and patience is meant to lead.

2:7 Paul cannot be saying that eternal life comes as a result of one's own achievements, since this runs counter to his own argument (3:20–21,28). What he is probably referring to are those good works that flow out of a right relationship with God. Notice he says that such people seek (not "deserve" or "have earned") the gifts that will be bestowed at the Second Coming.

2:8 The contrast is between self-seekers and God-seekers.

2:9 *affliction and distress.* The results of wrath and anger. *Greek.* Everyone who is not a Jew.

2:11 This is the point of his argument. The means by which one gains "wrath and indignation" (v. 8) or "eternal life" (v. 7) has nothing to do with national or racial heritage.

2:12 Everyone will be held accountable according to the knowledge they have. The Jews had the written Law; the Gentiles had their conscience (v. 15) and the revelation of nature (1:20).

2:13 This fact will be an awful blow to Jews. The Law is not, it turns out, a magic talisman that preserves those who hear it. It is by obeying the Law that people are blessed (James 1:22–25). *declared righteous.* Granted a verdict of acquittal.

2:14–15 Gentiles not only know about God from his creation, but their very consciences tell them that there is right and wrong (as is shown by the fact that some Gentiles do good).

2:15 *accuse or excuse.* The existence of inner moral conflict shows that Gentiles also know something of God's moral law.

2:16 *secret.* God's judgment is not based on outward appearances but upon what is in the heart (1 Sam. 16:7).

Jews: The Law and the Heart

Scripture Romans 2:17–29

LAST WEEK *The wrath and grace of a holy God was our focus in last week's session. We looked at how it is God's role to judge the sins of humanity and not ours, since none of us are innocent. We were also reminded that our response should be one of repentance and gratefulness for the kindness, restraint and patience of God. Today we are going to consider the emphasis that the Jews put on external measurements of spirituality and how we tend to do the same thing.*

 **Ice-Breaker** Connect With Your Group **(15 minutes)**

Many of the Jews in Paul's time had to spend most of their free time and devote their talents to following the Law as closely as possible. Take turns sharing some thoughts about your talents and time.

Leader
If you have new group members that need to get acquainted, remember to do all three Ice-Breaker questions. Be sure everyone gets a chance to participate.

1. In what field do you really excel? In what field would you like to excel?

    ○ Music.
    ○ Sports.
    ○ School.
    ○ Research.
    ○ Numbers/Math.
    ○ Administration.
    ○ People.
    ○ Other _____.

2. What was the most common thing your family did on the weekends when you were growing up?

3. What is your favorite thing to do with your free time?

Bible Study Read Scripture and Discuss (30 minutes)

We all have issues and problems that get us sidetracked sometimes. The Jews got very distracted by the Law. As we will read, they focused on the wrong thing—the outward appearance rather than the inward heart of man. Read Romans 2:17-29 and note how the Jews began to seek the praise of men, rather than God.

Leader
Select a member of the group ahead of time to read aloud the Scripture passage. Then discuss the Questions for Interaction, dividing into subgroups of three to six.

Jews: The Law and the Heart

[17]Now if you call yourself a Jew, and rest in the law, and boast in God, [18]and know His will, and approve the things that are superior, being instructed from the law, [19]and are convinced that you are a guide for the blind, a light to those in darkness, [20]an instructor of the ignorant, a teacher of the immature, having in the law the full expression of knowledge and truth— [21]you then, who teach another, do you not teach yourself? You who preach, "You must not steal"—do you steal? [22]You who say, "You must not commit adultery"—do you commit adultery? You who detest idols, do you rob their temples? [23]You who boast in the law, do you dishonor God by breaking the law? [24]For, as it is written: The name of God is blasphemed among the Gentiles because of you.

[25]For circumcision benefits you if you observe the law, but if you are a lawbreaker, your circumcision has become uncircumcision. [26]Therefore if an uncircumcised man keeps the law's requirements, will his uncircumcision not be counted as circumcision? [27]A man who is physically uncircumcised, but who fulfills the law, will judge you who are a lawbreaker in spite of having the letter of the law and circumcision. [28]For a person is not a Jew who is one outwardly, and true circumcision is not something visible in the flesh. [29]On the contrary, a person is a Jew who is one inwardly, and circumcision is of the heart—by the Spirit, not the letter. His praise is not from men but from God.

Romans 2:17-29

Questions for Interaction

1. What are some traditions in your family that you want to pass on to the generation that follows?

2. What does Paul accuse the Jews of being in this passage? If you were a Jew, how would you feel?

   ◯ Upset.
   ◯ Attacked.
   ◯ Found out.
   ◯ Other _____.

Leader
Refer to the Summary and Study Notes at the end of this session as needed. If 30 minutes is not enough time to answer all of the questions in this section, conclude the Bible Study by answering question 7.

3. From verses 17–20, what feelings did Paul's fellow Jews have about themselves? In contrast, how did their Gentile neighbors feel about them (vv. 21–24)?

4. How had the Jews missed the point of what circumcision was all about (vv. 25–29)?

5. What "spiritual customs" do you want to see continue with the generation that follows you? What "spiritual customs" have you abandoned that the previous generation still champions?

○ Music style.
○ Teaching/preaching.
○ Method of evangelism/discipleship.
○ Sunday school/small groups.
○ Lifestyle issues—movies, alcohol, outer appearance.
○ Other _____.

6. What custom or ritual do you have that needs to become less of a ritual and more of a matter of the heart?

7. What is God saying to you about your heart right now? What adjustments do you need to make to be more real with God and others about your faith?

Going Deeper   If your group has time and/or wants a challenge, go on to this question.

8. In contrast to physical circumcision, how is circumcision "of the heart" acquired, and what does it mean (v. 29; Deut. 10:16; 30:6; Jer. 4:4; 9:25–26)?

 Caring Time Apply the Lesson and Pray for One Another (15 minutes)

Bring your "circumcised" heart now to God and share your real needs and concerns in this time of sharing and prayer. After responding to the following questions, share prayer requests and pray for each other's needs.

Leader
Encourage everyone to participate in this important time and be sure that each group member is receiving prayer support. Continue to pray for the empty chair in the closing group prayer.

1. On a scale of 1 (superficial and shallow) to 10 (genuine and heartfelt), how would you describe your relationship with God this past week?

2. What can you do to make your worship more meaningful in the coming weeks?

3. How can this group pray for you and support you in making your faith more real and a part of every area of your life?

Notes on Romans 2:17-29

Summary: Paul now focuses on the self-righteous Jews who would protest that they at least were assured of God's favor (because they possessed God's law and bore the mark of circumcision). Paul argues in this section that neither the Law (vv. 17–24) nor circumcision (vv. 25–29) guarantees salvation. It is the internal work of God in our hearts.

2:17 *Jew.* This name was first used in Nehemiah 4:1. By Jesus' time it had come to assume a great significance for the people of Israel. To be a Jew was to be special; to be a Jew was to be a child of God. It is this intense nationalistic pride that Paul is attacking here, saying that it alone is insufficient to ensure salvation. *law.* This term is used in various ways. On the most basic level, it signified the set of laws given at the time of the Exodus (the Ten Commandments). The term could also refer to the laws contained in the first five books of the Old Testament (i.e., the Law of Moses). Or it could mean the whole Old Testament as well as its interpretation. In any case, the Jews felt special because they of all people had been singled out by God to receive his instructions on moral and ritual conduct—a fact that they felt guaranteed them favorable treatment by God on the Day of Judgment. *rest in the law.* This literally means to "rest upon the law"; to provide a sense that as a Jew one is indeed right with God.

2:19–20 These are the very terms the Jews would have used to describe their active and successful missionary work among the Gentiles during Paul's time. Although the Gentiles despised and ridiculed Judaism, they were also attracted by its purity in contrast to pagan worship. Paul uses these terms in an ironic sense.

2:21–23 Jews were noted for their high moral standards, so Paul may mean that they are guilty of these sins in the redefined sense given by Jesus (e.g., Matt. 5:27–28—even to look with lust at a woman is equivalent to adultery with her). Or he may be speaking in a racial sense, as in Malachi 3:8–9, where Israel as a nation is accused of robbing God of his tithe (see also Jer. 3:8). Probably, though, Paul means all this in quite a literal sense, since Jewish writers themselves catalog occurrences of stealing, etc. among religious leaders.

2:22 *rob their temples.* Apparently some Jews were not above robbing pagan shrines ("since such gods were not real anyway"). In Acts 19:37, the town clerk at Ephesus, in trying to quiet the mob, tells them that Paul has not been charged with robbing temples (a strange comment if Jews were never guilty of this behavior).

2:24 There was great contempt for Jews (mixed with curious attraction) for several reasons: Jews did not eat swine, they were not required to serve in the army, and they had their own courts. Jews were especially hated because of the contempt they showed toward other religions. Such hatred of Jews carried over to hatred for the God of Israel.

2:25 *circumcision.* This was the sign of the covenant with God (Gen. 17:1–14).

2:28–29 The Old Testament teaches in Deuteronomy 30:6 that true circumcision is not an outward, physical mark but an inward spiritual work by God. But Paul teaches that it is possible to neglect circumcision and still be counted as obedient to God's law. Paul's Jewish readers would certainly see this as a radical new teaching.

2:29 *circumcision is of the heart.* This fulfills "the spirit" of God's law instead of outward conformity to the Law. Some Jews followed the Law's regulation by being circumcised physically, but their hearts were not right with God (Isa. 29:13). Paul is calling them to be honest with God, and turn from sin toward God with their entire selves, internal as well as external.

God Is Faithful

Scripture Romans 3:1–8

LAST WEEK *What is the measure of true faith? Last week we focused on this question as we saw Paul address the Jews who were so caught up in the external measurement of spirituality that they missed out on a real relationship with God. We were reminded that often we tend to do the same thing, but that we need to concentrate on our inward spirituality and the condition of our hearts. Today we are going to look at the faithfulness of God and how he treats all people the same when it comes to sin and forgiveness.*

Ice-Breaker Connect With Your Group (15 minutes)

Our heritage and background can influence our lives in many ways. Many people celebrate certain days that are specific to their heritage, and some even travel to foreign countries in search of information about their ancestors. Take turns sharing your unique background with the group.

1. Where are your ancestors from? How much do you know about them?

2. What traditions do you celebrate that are specific to your heritage?

3. Among your relatives, who comes closest to being the family's spiritual "patriarch"?

Leader
Choose one or two of the Ice-Breaker questions. If you have a new group member you may want to do all three. Remember to stick closely to the three-part agenda and the time allowed for each segment.

Bible Study Read Scripture and Discuss (30 minutes)

Leader
Have a member of the group, selected ahead of time, read aloud the Scripture passage. Then discuss the Questions for Interaction, dividing into subgroups of three to six.

The Jews are God's chosen people. Does that give them special grace to sin or not to take God's judgment as seriously as Gentiles? As we are about to read, God is faithful in the treatment of sin and willing to forgive all people. Read Romans 3:1–8 and note how God is truth itself.

God Is Faithful

3 So what advantage does the Jew have? Or what is the benefit of circumcision? [2]Considerable in every way. First, they were entrusted with the spoken words of God. [3]What then? If some did not believe, will their unbelief cancel God's faithfulness? [4]Absolutely not! God must be true, but everyone is a liar, as it is written:

> That You may be justified in Your words
> and triumph when You judge.

[5]But if our unrighteousness highlights God's righteousness, what are we to say? I use a human argument: Is God unrighteous to inflict wrath? [6]Absolutely not! Otherwise, how will God judge the world? [7]But if by my lie God's truth is amplified to His glory, why am I also still judged as a sinner? [8]And why not say, just as some people slanderously claim we say, "Let us do evil so that good may come"? Their condemnation is deserved!

Romans 3:1–8

Questions for Interaction

Leader
Refer to the Summary and Study Notes at the end of this session as needed. If 30 minutes is not enough time to answer all of the questions in this section, conclude the Bible Study by answering question 7.

1. Who was the disciplinarian in your family?

   ○ Mom.
   ○ Dad.
   ○ Grandparent.
   ○ Other _____.

2. What are the advantages of growing up in a Christian environment? What are the potential disadvantages?

3. What are the three questions asked in verses 1–6? How does Paul answer them?

4. How did the Jews define "unrighteousness" or sin? How does society define sin? How do you define sin? How does God define sin?

5. How would you respond to someone who casually says, "It's okay to lie because all I have to do is ask God for forgiveness and he will forgive me?"

6. From your experience, do you find it necessary for someone to realize a need for God's grace and forgiveness before they will fully appreciate that Christ died for them?

7. When did you first become aware of your sinfulness and need for God? What does God's faithfulness and forgiveness mean to you in your daily life?

Going Deeper   If your group has time and/or wants a challenge, go on to this question.

8. Does God give special recognition to the Jews? Why or why not?

Caring Time Apply the Lesson and Pray for One Another (15 minutes)

Come together now for a time of prayer, remembering that God is faithful to all of his promises. After sharing your responses to the questions below, close by praying for one another and the concerns that have been shared.

Leader
Be sure to save at least 15 minutes for this time of prayer and encouragement. Continue to encourage group members to invite new people to the group.

1. What season are you experiencing in your spiritual life right now?

   ○ The warmth of summer.
   ○ The dead of winter.
   ○ The new life of spring.
   ○ The changes of fall.

2. How are you doing at forgiving those who sin against you? Is there someone you need to go to this week to make things right?

3. What is something God is challenging you to do from this study of Romans?

NEXT WEEK *Today we looked at the faithfulness of God and how he treats all people the same when it comes to sin and forgiveness. We were encouraged to make things right with someone we have wronged or someone who has hurt us. In the coming week, pray for and reach out to that person you need to forgive. Next week we will look at the sins of the human race and Christ's sacrifice for those sins.*

Summary: The dialogue between Paul and his audience comes out into the open now via a series of questions and answers. There is a terseness and "Jewishness" to this section that makes it somewhat baffling at first glance. Three potential objections to his argument in chapter 2 are raised and dealt with in: (a) vv. 1–2, (b) vv. 3–4 and (c) vv. 5–8.

3:1 *what advantage.* Paul answers the question, "Do you really mean, as you seem to argue in chapter 2, that there is no significant difference between a Jew and a Gentile?" Such a question arose out of an accurate understanding that God had set Israel apart from all other nations. This is not a trivial charge. Can God's dealings with his people be trusted? Is God faithful? Is the Old Testament accurate? If there is no value to circumcision or advantage to being the covenant people (Jews), then the reliability of God and his Word seems to be called into question. The whole question of Israel's place in God's plan will be considered in depth in chapters 9–11. At this point, it is sufficient to note that the Jews, in seeing themselves as a people of special privilege, had forgotten that they were also charged with special responsibility. It is they who had opted out of active participation in God's unfolding plan.

3:2 *Considerable in every way.* This reply is unexpected, given what Paul said in chapter 2. It might have been assumed that he would reply: "Jews have no advantage." But this would not be accurate. They had a preeminent place in God's plan. It was through them that God worked out the redemption of the world in his Son Jesus, who was a Jew. Still, while this was a decided advantage, it was never intended to be the basis on which Jews would be excluded from facing judgment. *First.* Paul does not complete his list. There is no "second," "third," etc. His argument takes another direction. In 9:4–5, however, he does give other advantages. *words of God.* It is an enormous advantage to have known the mind and will of God.

3:3 *some.* In relative terms, some Jews are more faithful than others (just as in 2:14–15, Paul

notes that some Gentiles do by nature what the Law requires). This idea of the "faithful remnant" is picked up again in chapters 9–11. Still, this relative goodness makes no difference ultimately in people's standing before God (3:9). An objection is raised: "So what that some were faithless? God surely is not going to hold that against all of Israel, and himself prove to be unfaithful by breaking his promise to the Jews!"

3:4 Paul answers, "Certainly not! Even if every single person were a liar, God remains true" (alluding to the words of Psalm 116:11). Then he quotes Psalm 51:4b, where this truth is demonstrated.

3:5 The next objection is repeated twice in verses 5 and 7: "How can I be found at fault when, because of my evil, God's truth is allowed to shine forth more clearly?"

3:6 Paul replies that if this were true and God was not allowed to judge sin, the moral fabric of the universe would be in jeopardy. If God is not fair, justice could not prevail. "But, in fact," he says (v. 8), "this assertion is really only slander and is to be condemned." The implication is that those who have experienced justification by faith find that God's love draws them to righteous living, not to unlimited sinning. This charge is dealt with more thoroughly in Romans 6:1–2.

3:8 *some people slanderously claim.* Some people twisted Paul's emphasis on God's grace to say that sinning was good in that it allowed God more opportunity to be gracious! Paul vehemently denies this.

Man's Problem and God's Solution

Scripture Romans 3:9–31

LAST WEEK *Last week we looked at the faithfulness of God and how he is the source of all truth. Because of his righteousness, he treats all people the same when it comes to sin and forgiveness. Since God is faithful to forgive, we also need to forgive those who have wronged or hurt us. Today we will look at how all have sinned and need atonement for those sins through Christ's sacrifice on the cross. We will remember how awesome his grace is to cleanse us from our sin.*

Ice-Breaker Connect With Your Group (15 minutes)

Sometimes we get in situations where we really need some help! Without Jesus' help and sacrifice we would all be lost. Take turns sharing how you have needed or given help.

1. What is the most dramatic rescue you've been involved in or witnessed (on TV or in person)?

2. When have you taken the heat for something you didn't do?

3. Who is someone in your life that made sacrifices so you could have a better life? What did that person do?

Leader
Introduce and welcome new group members. If there are no new members, choose one or two of the Ice-Breaker questions to get started. If there are new members, then discuss all three.

Bible Study Read Scripture and Discuss (30 minutes)

Guilt is a huge barrier that keeps many from ever knowing true forgiveness in their life. Our sin has serious consequences and no one is exempt. But God provided a way for us to be free from guilt and the burden of sin through the sacrificial act of Jesus on the cross. Read Romans 3:9–31 and note how the Law and grace work together.

Leader
Select a member of the group ahead of time to read aloud the Scripture passage. Then discuss the Questions for Interaction, dividing into subgroups of three to six.

Man's Problem and God's Solution

[9]What then? Are we any better? Not at all! For we have previously charged that both Jews and Gentiles are all under sin, [10] as it is written:

There is no one righteous, not even one;
[11]there is no one who understands,
there is no one who seeks God.
[12]All have turned away,
together they have become useless;
there is no one who does good,
there is not even one.
[13]Their throat is an open grave;
they deceive with their tongues.
Vipers' venom is under their lips.
[14]Their mouth is full of cursing and bitterness.
[15]Their feet are swift to shed blood;
[16]ruin and wretchedness are in their paths,
[17]and the path of peace they have not known.
[18]There is no fear of God before their eyes.

[19]Now we know that whatever the law says speaks to those who are subject to the law, so that every mouth may be shut and the whole world may become subject to God's judgment. [20]For no flesh will be justified in His sight by the works of the law, for through the law comes the knowledge of sin.

[21]But now, apart from the law, God's righteousness has been revealed—attested by the Law and the Prophets [22]—that is, God's righteousness through faith in Jesus Christ, to all who believe, since there is no distinction. [23]For all have sinned and fall short of the glory of God. [24]They are justified freely by His grace through the redemption that is in Christ Jesus. [25]God presented Him as a propitiation through faith in His blood, to demonstrate His righteousness, because in His restraint God passed over the sins previously committed. [26]He presented Him to demonstrate His righteousness at the present time, so that He would be righteous and declare righteous the one who has faith in Jesus.

[27]Where then is boasting? It is excluded. By what kind of law? By one of works? No, on the contrary, by a law of faith. [28]For we conclude that a man is justified by faith apart from works of law. [29]Or is God for Jews only? Is He not also for Gentiles? Yes, for Gentiles too, [30]since there is one God who will justify the circumcised by faith and the uncircumcised through faith. [31]Do we then cancel the law through faith? Absolutely not! On the contrary, we uphold the law.

Romans 3:9–31

Questions for Interaction

1. If you could eliminate any laws from your state, what would you eliminate? What law would you add?

   - ○ Speed limits on the freeways.
   - ○ Wearing seatbelts.
   - ○ Smoking in public places.
   - ○ Stricter gun control.
   - ○ Other _____.

Leader
Refer to the Summary and Study Notes at the end of this session as needed. If 30 minutes is not enough time to answer all of the questions in this section, conclude the Bible Study by answering question 7.

2. How would your friends who are unfamiliar with church react to verses 10–18, 23?

3. With the coming of Christ to bring salvation, does the Law become invalid? Why or why not? What does the Law reveal about human beings?

4. How did the action by God on behalf of all mankind level the playing field between Jew and Gentile?

5. What do the words "justified" and "redemption" mean (v. 24)? What do they mean to you personally?

6. How would you communicate the concept of undeserving grace to someone who is hung up with doing good works to get into heaven? How could you relate this truth from your own application in life?

7. What impact does the message of God's grace have on your life right now? How often do you thank God for this wonderful gift?

Going Deeper   If your group has time and/or wants a challenge, go on to this question.

8. What is the meaning of the phrase in verse 25, "God passed over the sins previously committed?" What value did this act of God give to the work of salvation by Christ?

♥ Caring Time Apply the Lesson and Pray for One Another (15 minutes)

Take some time now to pray for one another, remembering to thank God for his wonderful gift of grace. Begin by sharing your responses to the following questions. Then share prayer requests and close with prayer.

1. On a scale of 1 (not at all) to 10 (completely fulfilled), how would you rate the way your spiritual needs are being met at this point in your life? How can this group help?

2. What is something you would like to thank God for in your life?

3. Who do you know that needs to hear this message of grace so that we can pray for them?

Leader
Continue to encourage group members to invite new people to the group. Remind everyone that this group is for learning and sharing, but also for reaching out to others. Close the group prayer by thanking God for each member and for this time together.

NEXT WEEK *Today we looked at how "all have sinned and fall short of the glory of God" (v. 23). We were reminded of Christ's sacrifice for those sins and how awesome God's grace is to cleanse us from our sin. In the coming week, continue to pray for the person you mentioned in question #3 in the Caring Time. Look for opportunities to share God's grace with that person. Next week we will explore the power of faith as the foundational component for receiving salvation. We will be encouraged by the trust that Abraham placed in God when things appeared most hopeless.*

Notes on Romans 3:9-31

Summary: In rabbinic fashion, Paul strings together various Old Testament verses drawn mainly from the Psalms, all of which add up to a frightening description of human nature. The point of these verses is clear: all people, be they Jew or Gentile, are under sin's power. This is seen in the fact that no one seeks God and his ways (vv. 10–12); their very words condemn them (vv. 13–14), as do their violent ways (vv. 15–18). Some have called verses 21–31 the greatest passage Paul ever wrote. It is the doctrinal center of the book of Romans. In it, Paul explains how right standing before God comes to a humanity that is hopelessly alienated from God. This new reality is so profound that a single word or phrase cannot capture its essence. Instead, Paul uses three metaphors to describe it. From the law court, he draws the idea of justification; from the slave market, the concept of redemption; and from the temple, the truth of an atoning sacrifice.

3:9 The questions in verse 1 are basically repeated, but now a different answer is given because Paul has a different distinction in mind. In verse 2 he admits that the Jews do have an advantage over the Gentiles. They have God's words. They know God's plan and God's will. But here he says this does not translate into an absolute guarantee of God's favor. *Are we any better?* This is one word in Greek, and carries the idea of "being superior to," "surpassing" and "excelling." *under sin.* Under the authority of sin. Paul is not thinking here about individual sins that a person commits, but rather about the way that sin controls people.

3:10 *righteous.* This word is used in two ways: no one has right standing before God and no one lives a moral life.

3:13–14 *throat/tongues/lips/mouth.* All these are meant to describe deceptive speech.

3:15–18 Verses 15–17 (Isaiah 59:7–8) recount the violent nature of human deeds, while the whole poem is climaxed by verse 18 which is a quote of the Greek version of Psalm 36:1b.

3:19 Paul answers one last possible objection: "Sure, we know those verses. They refer to the Gentiles." "No," Paul replies here, "that which is in the Old Testament is directed to those who possess the Old Testament. These verses describe you too!" In other words, the Jews' very advantage (v. 2) is the source of their condemnation. In having the "words of God," the Jews, of all people, should know their sin (and hence their guilt) before God

3:20 Once again Paul turns to the Old Testament to clinch his case. Here he echoes (though does not directly quote) Psalm 143:2b. The function of the Law, rather than being a shield against God's wrath, is to make people aware of their sin. Once it has done that, its power is expended. It cannot hide a

person from God's action on the Day of Judgment.

3:21 *But now.* The turning point in the argument; a new factor enters the picture. Paul moves from the revelation of God's wrath (1:18) to the revelation of God's righteousness. *apart from the law.* God's righteousness as revealed by the Law leads only to wrath (4:15), but God's righteousness as now revealed in Jesus Christ leads to right standing before him. *God's righteousness.* Righteousness is an attribute of God that individuals come to know via his saving activity, through which they gain the status of being counted righteous before him. *the Law and the Prophets.* The Old Testament, if rightly understood, does contain such a message. Paul has already used Habakkuk 2:4 when first describing the Gospel (1:17).

3:22 *faith.* Individuals are not counted as righteous because of faith, as if it were an attitude on their part that forces God to accept them. Rather, they are counted as righteous (justified) because of grace through (or "on the basis of") faith. Faith, then, is a profound trust and hope in God's work in Christ. Faith is the opposite of works. Works give people a sense of self-confidence, because they assume (falsely) that their religious and moral activities will cause God to pronounce them justified. *in Jesus Christ.* Paul writes not about faith in general (a vague feeling that "all will turn out well"), but about faith in a specific person, Jesus Christ. *to all.* The Gospel is for Jew and Gentile alike.

3:23 *fall short.* The picture is of arrows that have failed to reach their target. Likewise, humanity has failed to live up to God's standards. *glory of God.* This is God's divine splendor, which is reflected in the Law.

3:24 *justified.* This is a word drawn from the law court. The image is of humanity on trial before God. Those who keep the Law perfectly will be declared innocent because they are innocent (2:1). The problem is that Paul has just shown that no one is innocent! But now through Christ, God has forgiven individuals their sins, and they are treated as if they were innocent. To be justified is to be granted acquittal on the Day of Judgment. That a bad person would be reckoned as if he or she were good was utterly shocking to the Jew (Ex. 23:7; Prov. 17:15). Such assurance of acquittal, coming as it does at the beginning of the Christian life (the Jew hoped for acquittal at the end of life), brings a great sense of personal freedom, since one is released from the nagging questions: Am I good enough? Will I merit heaven? Now, by grace, individuals are pronounced "righteous" and are freed to do good works out of love for God, not out of fear of his wrath. *redemption.* This refers to the act of buying the freedom of a slave—in this case, a slave in bondage to sin (Mark 10:45; 1 Peter 1:18–19). There are rich Old Testament overtones to this word. Israel was enslaved to Egypt and under the power of Pharaoh and thus in need of redemption (Deut. 7:8). It is God who redeemed them from their bondage. In the same way, Christ secured the release of humanity from the power of sin.

3:25 *a propitiation.* The image now shifts to the temple and the Old Testament system of sacrifice. The word used here is used in the Greek version of the Old Testament for the "mercy seat"—the golden slab that covered the ark in the holiest place of the temple. It was visited once a year on the Day of Atonement by the high priest, who sprinkled on it the blood of sacrifice to secure, symbolically, forgiveness for the sins of the people (Lev. 16). Christ's death is the ultimate, final and complete sacrifice for sin.

Christ is the victim who takes upon himself the wrath due because of humanity's sin. Christ took upon himself the full weight of God's wrath which sinful humanity deserved. *His blood.* In terms of atonement, the importance of Jesus' death was that his blood was offered to God as a sacrifice. Since it is by entrusting oneself to Jesus as the sacrifice that one is justified and redeemed, "his blood" became a shorthand way of referring to all the meaning implied in Christ's sacrificial death. *passed over.* God's "overlooking" of sin prior to Christ's coming might have been understood as indicating that God was not seriously opposed to sin. In fact, the reason for his forbearance was that one day Christ would bear all such sin on the cross (Isa. 53:6).

3:26 *righteousness at the present time.* The sacrificial death of Christ demonstrates God's justice in two ways: First, by vindicating Jesus—he has taken sin so seriously that God sent his own Son to die. Second, by showing a whole new way of living that Christ's sacrifice has opened up for humanity.

3:27 *boasting.* His statement of the Good News complete, Paul now addresses Jewish resistance. It's all right to boast about what God has done, but not about one's own actions, especially as if these were the basis for one's salvation.

3:31 Paul might have been expected to say that faith did nullify the Law, because he had shown that the Law was not effective if understood as a way of putting people right with God. What he seems to have in mind here is that, understood as a revelation of God's will, the Law is certainly still valid.

The Power of Faith

Scripture Romans 4:1–25

LAST WEEK *In last week's session, we discussed how "all have sinned and fall short of the glory of God" (3:23). We were reminded that only through God's grace and Christ's sacrificial death can we be cleansed from our sins. We also prayed for our friends who have yet to accept this truth by faith. Today we are going to explore the power of faith as the foundational component for receiving salvation. We will be encouraged by the incredible trust Abraham placed in God when it seemed that all was hopeless.*

Ice-Breaker Connect With Your Group (15 minutes)

The faith we have is tested every day in many small, and sometimes large, ways. Abraham's faith was especially tested when he had grown old and still did not have the son God had promised him. Take turns sharing some of your experiences and thoughts on faith.

Leader
Choose one, two or all three of the Ice-Breaker questions. Be sure to welcome and introduce new group members.

1. What "great deal" have you had faith in, only to discover it was a scam that promised something for nothing?

2. In what situation do you have a hard time having faith?

   ○ When I'm flying.
   ○ When I need surgery.
   ○ When I have to give a speech.
   ○ When I'm teaching my teenager how to drive.
   ○ Other _____.

3. Who is someone you admire with a lot of faith?

Bible Study Read Scripture and Discuss (30 minutes)

The faith of Abraham is sometimes hard to imagine when we look at the obstacles he faced. He and his wife, Sarah, were very old and God still hadn't granted them a son. But Abraham never wavered and he continued to hold on for many years to the promises that God had given him, trusting in God's perfect timing. Read Romans 4:1–25 and take note of the blessings that result from faith.

Leader
Ask two members of the group, selected ahead of time, to read aloud the Scripture passage. Then have the group divide into subgroups of three to six to discuss the Questions for Interaction.

The Power of Faith

Reader One: 4 What then can we say that Abraham, our forefather according to the flesh, has found? [2]If Abraham was justified by works, then he has something to brag about—but not before God. [3]For what does the Scripture say?

Abraham believed God,
and it was credited to him for righteousness.

[4]Now to the one who works, pay is not considered as a gift, but as something owed. [5]But to the one who does not work, but believes on Him who declares righteous the ungodly, his faith is credited for righteousness.

Reader Two: [6]Likewise, David also speaks of the blessing of the man to whom God credits righteousness apart from works:

[7]How happy those whose lawless acts are forgiven
and whose sins are covered!
[8]How happy the man whom
the Lord will never charge with sin!

Reader One: [9]Is this blessing only for the circumcised, then? Or is it also for the uncircumcised? For we say, Faith was credited to Abraham for righteousness. [10]How then was it credited—while he was circumcised, or uncircumcised? Not while he was circumcised, but uncircumcised. [11]And he received the sign of circumcision as a seal of the righteousness that he had by faith while still uncircumcised. This was to make him the father of all who believe but are not circumcised, so that righteousness may be credited to them also. [12]And he became the father of the circumcised, not only to those who are circumcised, but also to those who follow in the footsteps of the faith our father Abraham had while still uncircumcised.

Reader Two: [13]For the promise to Abraham or to his descendants that he would inherit the world was not through the law, but through the righteousness that comes by faith. [14]If those who are of the law are heirs, faith is made empty and the promise is canceled. [15]For the law produces wrath; but where there is no law, there is no transgression.

Reader One: [16]This is why the promise is by faith, so that it may be according to grace, to guarantee it to all the descendants—not only to those who are of the law, but also to those who are of Abraham's faith. He is the father of us all [17]in God's sight. As it is written: I have made you the father of many nations. He believed in God, who gives life to the dead and calls things into existence that do not exist. [18]Against hope, with hope he believed, so that he became the father of many nations, according to what had been spoken: So will your descendants be. [19]He considered his own body to be already dead (since he was about a hundred years old), and the deadness of Sarah's womb, without weakening in the faith. [20]He did not waver in unbelief at God's promise, but was strengthened in his faith and gave glory to God, [21]because he was fully convinced that what He had promised He was also able to perform. [22]Therefore, it was credited to him for righteousness. [23]Now it was credited to him was not written for Abraham alone, [24]but also for us. It will be credited to us who believe in Him who raised Jesus our Lord from the dead. [25]He was delivered up for our trespasses and raised for our justification.

Romans 4:1–25

Questions for Interaction

Leader
Refer to the Summary and Study Notes at the end of this session as needed. If 30 minutes is not enough time to answer all of the questions in this section, conclude the Bible Study by answering questions 6 and 7.

1. What truth or concept of Christianity do you have a hard time believing? What about it do you find hard to believe?

   ○ God can forgive all sins.
   ○ The existence of heaven or hell.
   ○ Jesus coming back again.
   ○ Humanity has free will.
   ○ God allows evil and suffering.
   ○ Other _____.

2. How do you feel when you receive an unexpected gift from someone? Is there a difference in the way you feel when you receive wages from your job? Why?

3. On the surface, what "qualifications" would seem to make Abraham an example of righteousness?

4. What are some of the facts that support Paul's case that Abraham was said to be righteous solely because of his faith in the promise of God?

5. What was Paul's conclusion about how this supported the good news of Jesus Christ (vv. 23–25)?

6. When have you had to hope against hope? What fears and doubts about God's promises did you struggle with?

7. Why is it hard for us to trust God at the level Abraham did? Where do you need to exercise more faith in God in your life right now?

8. In some religions, forgiveness or grace as a free gift is a foreign concept. You "earn" your way to heaven by doing good deeds. What would have happened to Christianity if Paul had given in on the issue of circumcision?

 **Caring Time** Apply the Lesson and Pray for One Another **(15 minutes)**

Help each other now to grow in faith by supporting one another in a time of sharing and prayer. Take turns sharing your responses to these questions before closing in a group prayer.

1. On a scale of 1 (mustard seed) to 10 (mountain moving), how would you rate your faith this past week?

2. What are some of the many promises God has given to those who follow him? Which promise do you need to hold on to right now in your life? Which one do you need to encourage someone else with right now?

3. Recall the comments that group members mentioned back in questions 6 and 7. How can you encourage one another?

Leader
Have you started working with your group about their mission—perhaps by sharing the dream of multiplying into two groups by the end of this study of Book 1 of Romans?

NEXT WEEK *Today we explored the power of faith as the foundational component for receiving salvation. We were encouraged by Abraham's example of placing his trust in God's promises, even when all seemed hopeless. In the coming week, pick two or three of God's promises found in Romans regarding faith and read them daily. (Work on memorizing them, too!) Next week we will look at the peace we have with God because of Jesus.*

Summary: Paul writes that his teaching in Romans 3:21–26 about how one is declared righteous before God (i.e., justified) is in accord with the Old Testament Scriptures (3:21). In this passage he proves this by examining the case of Abraham and showing that the father of the Jewish race was justified by faith and not by anything he did (vv. 1–8), not even by circumcision (vv. 9–12) or by keeping the Law (vv. 13–15). Paul shows that justification by faith is not heresy, but the clear intent of the Old Testament when correctly read.

4:1 *Abraham.* As the first patriarch and thus the founder of the Jewish nation, all Jews revered Abraham. They knew him to be God's friend (Isa. 41:8) who willingly set out on a long pilgrimage at God's command, who endured many trials, and who was even willing to give up to God his most precious possession—his son, Isaac.

4:2 *brag.* Paul stated that no one has the right to boast because justification is by faith, not by works (3:27). First-century Jewish thought would have pointed to Abraham in objecting to that assertion. According to one document: "Abraham was perfect in all his deeds with the Lord and well-pleasing in righteousness all the days of his life." So if Paul can show that even Abraham had no cause to glory, then bragging by everyone else would be excluded.

4:5 declares righteous the ungodly. That God would do this contradicts Jewish expectations. God was supposed to condemn the guilty (Ex. 23:7). Paul makes this point because everyone would then agree that acquitting the guilty could only be seen as an act of grace, not as a response by God to good works. God was able to justify the wicked because of the future sacrifice of the Messiah (Isa. 53:4–12; John 8:56). ***faith.*** Two views of faith are in contention. The Jews saw faith as a definite activity, as faithful action in accordance with God's will. Thus they understood that God responded to Abraham's

faith by declaring him "righteous." In contrast, Paul understood faith in exactly opposite terms, as a person's response to God's action (1:17; 3:21–26).

4:6–8 David, the other great national hero, is used as an example of the relief that comes from unmerited divine pardon.

4:11 *seal.* Circumcision is merely the external sign or token of the righteous status conferred by God on Abraham. ***father.*** Jews believed Abraham was the father of their race. In fact, Paul argues he is really the father of believing Gentiles and is only the father of those Jews who believe! This would have been a devastating critique to the Jews—an absolute reversal of what they held.

4:14 If Abraham's heirs were those who kept the Law, God's promise would be null and void, because there would be no heirs since no one keeps the Law (Gal. 3:10–14).

4:16 *promise.* Paul could have used two possible Greek words. The first denotes a promise that is conditional: "You do this and I promise to do that." The second word, which he actually uses in this verse, describes an unconditional promise made out of the generosity of one's heart. God's promise (probably meaning the whole plan of salvation) is a gift of grace, not a contract with certain obligations. ***by faith.*** By its very notion, a person can do nothing but wait for the fulfillment of a promised inheritance.

4:17 Since the promise to Abraham in Genesis is in the plural, it was not just the Jewish nation God had in mind as Abraham's descendants. *life to the dead.* As when God gave Abraham and Sarah the ability to have a child, although biologically this was impossible (v. 19).

4:18 *Against hope.* Many years had passed after God first promised heirs to Abraham in Genesis 12:2, and still Abraham trusted.

4:24–25 Paul concludes his case by focusing on what Jesus did: Individuals are granted right standing with God because of their trust in the death and resurrection of Jesus.

Peace With God

Scripture Romans 5:1–11

LAST WEEK *Abraham's example of faith in God's promises was discussed last week, as we explored the power of faith as the foundational component for receiving salvation. We were reminded that God's promises are still true today and we can hold on to them in times of doubt. Today we will look at three blessings that come to those who believe in Jesus. We will also look at the part that afflictions play in experiencing God's eternal hope.*

Ice-Breaker Connect With Your Group (15 minutes)

Leader
Welcome and introduce new group members. Choose one, two or all three Ice-Breaker questions, depending on your group's needs.

We all have our ups and downs in this life. No matter what our circumstances, though, we can turn to God to find peace and joy in our salvation. Take turns sharing with the group some of the ups and downs of your life.

1. What has been the happiest moment of your life to date? Describe your feelings at that moment.

   ○ My wedding day.
   ○ The birth of a child.
   ○ The day I became a follower of Christ.
   ○ The moment I realized what my purpose is in life.
   ○ Other _____.

2. What is a low point that you have experienced in life? Describe your feelings at that moment.

3. What are you most looking forward to in the future?

Bible Study Read Scripture and Discuss (30 minutes)

Leader
Select a member of the group ahead of time to read aloud the Scripture passage. Then discuss the Questions for Interaction, dividing into subgroups of three to six.

Peace, grace and hope are promised to those who believe in Jesus Christ. Yet the afflictions and suffering that invade our lives can make these promises seem far in the distance. But God proves his own love for us and uses our afflictions to develop us into the kind of people he wants us to be. Read Romans 5:1–11 and note the many reasons to be thankful that we follow Christ.

Peace With God

5 Therefore, since we have been declared righteous by faith, we have peace with God through our Lord Jesus Christ. [2]Also through Him, we have obtained access by faith into this grace in which we stand, and we rejoice in the hope of the glory of God. [3]And not only that, but we also rejoice in our afflictions, because we know that affliction produces endurance, [4]endurance produces proven character, and proven character produces hope. [5]This hope does not disappoint, because God's love has been poured out in our hearts through the Holy Spirit who was given to us.

[6]For while we were still helpless, at the appointed moment, Christ died for the ungodly. [7]For rarely will someone die for a just person—though for a good person perhaps someone might even dare to die. [8]But God proves His own love for us in that while we were still sinners Christ died for us! [9]Much more then, since we have now been declared righteous by His blood, we will be saved through Him from wrath. [10]For if, while we were enemies, we were reconciled to God through the death of His Son, then how much more, having been reconciled, will we be saved by His life! [11]And not only that, but we also rejoice in God through our Lord Jesus Christ, through whom we have now received reconciliation.

Romans 5:1–11

Questions for Interaction

Leader
Refer to the Summary and Study Notes at the end of this session as needed. If 30 minutes is not enough time to answer all of the questions in this section, conclude the Bible Study by answering question 7.

1. What do you do to wind down, release stress and relax?

   ○ Read a good book.
   ○ Take a walk.
   ○ Listen to music.
   ○ Watch TV.
   ○ Be with my family.
   ○ Other _____.

2. What kind of hope is Paul writing about in verses 2 and 5? How is this hope different than the "wishful hope" we sometimes use in our daily conversations?

3. Paul wrote that the journey of hope would involve afflictions, which produce endurance and character, resulting in hope. When have you seen or experienced suffering that led to the hope Paul writes about?

4. How does one rejoice in afflictions and rejoice in God? What does being "saved by His life," (v. 10) mean to you?

5. What is the simplicity of the Gospel message in verses 8–10? When did you experience this?

6. Through Jesus we receive reconciliation with God. In what relationship do you need to experience reconciliation?

    ○ With God.
    ○ With my family.
    ○ With a friend.
    ○ With coworkers.
    ○ Other _____.

7. As followers of Christ we are the recipients of peace, grace and hope. What do these words mean to you? Which one do you need the most in your life right now?

Going Deeper   If your group has time and/or wants a challenge, go on to this question.

8. What role does the Holy Spirit play in the life development process found in verses 3 and 4?

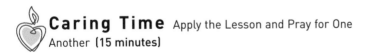 **Caring Time** Apply the Lesson and Pray for One Another (15 minutes)

For us to enjoy the blessings that are ours in Christ we need more than study—we need support and encouragement. This is your time to give that to each other. Share your responses to the following questions before closing in prayer.

Leader
Have you identified someone in the group who could be a leader for a new small group when your group divides? How could you encourage and mentor that person?

1. What do you look forward to the most about these meetings?

2. What is something you can do in the coming week to spread some peace to others?

3. Look around your group. Who comes to mind when you think of peace? Tell them. Who comes to mind when you think of grace? Tell them. Do the same for hope.

NEXT WEEK *Today we looked at the blessings of peace, grace and hope that come to those who believe in Jesus. We also considered the role that afflictions play in learning to lean on God's eternal hope. In the coming week, remember to reflect God's peace in your relationships with others and to bear your sufferings with a heart of thanksgiving. Next week we will look at Adam's influence on the human race and the devastating consequences. We will compare that with Christ's influence on the human race and his life-giving consequences.*

Notes on Romans 5:1-11

Summary: Having explained God's way of justifying sinners and establishing that this is in harmony with Old Testament teaching, Paul now identifies the three blessings that occur to those justified by faith: peace, grace and hope. This is a transitional passage that serves to introduce the themes of the next major section of Romans (chapters 5–8), much as 1:16–17 introduced the themes of 1:18–4:25. Again, Paul will first establish the negative in 5:12–7:25 (as he did in 1:18–3:20), and then go on to expound the positive in 8:1–39 (as he did in 3:21–4:25).

5:1 *peace.* What is in view is not some sort of inner experience of harmony, but rather the objective fact of a new relationship with God. The root image is of war. Those who were in rebellion against God, their rightful king, are now reconciled to him through Christ; the enmity is over. This is the basis for the Christian's access to God's grace and hope for the future. Peace in the Bible is a comprehensive term describing the total blessing of salvation.

5:2 *access.* This word is used to describe ushering someone into the presence of royalty. *grace.* To be at peace with God is to come into the sphere of his grace and thus experience the new kind of life that will be described in 5:12–8:39. *hope.* This is a sure sense of confidence based on the fact of justification. *glory of God.* That for which humans were created and from which they have fallen, but which they will someday experience again. The future destiny of humankind is to be glorified; i.e., to share in this aspect of God's nature.

5:3 *afflictions.* Literally, "pressure" or "tribulation." What is in view is not sorrow or pain, but the negative reaction of an unbelieving world. In New Testament times, suffering was the normal and expected lot of Christians (Acts 14:22). On one hand, their refusal to engage in immoral or idolatrous practices was seen as disloyalty to the nation or disdain of the culture. On the other hand, they were blamed falsely when things went wrong and so suffered persecution as scapegoats. Thus, suffering was seen as a sign of true Christianity (2 Thess. 1:4–5). *endurance.* Fortitude or perseverance. The word describes the active overcoming of misfortune, rather than mere passive acceptance.

5:4 *character.* A word used of metal that has been so heated by fire that all the impurities have been burned out. *hope.* The confidence, born out of suffering, that God is indeed transforming one's character, and that he will keep on until one is glorified.

5:5 The presence of the Holy Spirit, given to believers as an expression of God's love, is the guarantee that one's hope is secure.

5:9 *Much more then.* These two contrasts (being declared righteous and saved from God's wrath) accent the richness of God's salvation experienced by those who entrust themselves to Christ who died and now lives again on their behalf. *wrath.* Believers are released from anxiety about the outcome of the Day of Judgment (1 Thess. 1:10; 5:9).

5:9–10 *declared righteous/reconciled.* Two different metaphors used to describe the same realities. Being declared righteous puts an end to legal contention with God the Judge. Reconciliation puts an end to rebellion against God the King. Lost status is restored; lost access is reopened.

5:10 *saved by His life.* The contrast is between the death of Christ that makes reconciliation (justification) possible, and the resurrection life of Christ as a result of his working in believers to effect their sanctification (salvation).

A Comparison Between Adam and Christ

Scripture Romans 5:12–21

LAST WEEK *Last week we looked at the blessings of peace, grace, and hope that come to those who believe in Jesus. We also considered the role that afflictions play in helping to develop our character and experience God's eternal hope. Today we will look at Adam's influence on the human race and the devastating consequences. We will compare that with Christ's influence on the human race and his life-giving consequences.*

Ice-Breaker Connect With Your Group (15 minutes)

There are many people who influence us in our lifetime. Some may be close family members and mentors; others may be historical figures or celebrities we will never meet. Share some of your thoughts about people who have influenced you.

Leader
Choose one or two of the Ice-Breaker questions. If you have a new group member you may want to do all three. Remember to stick to the three-part agenda and the time allowed for each segment.

1. Who do people say you are more like, your mom or your dad?

2. If you could trade places with anyone for one month, what specific person from which one of the following fields would you be?

   ○ Actor.
   ○ Musician.
   ○ Athlete.
   ○ Politician.
   ○ Millionaire.
   ○ Other _____.

3. Who do you know that is in heaven now that you would really like to see again?

📖 Bible Study Read Scripture and Discuss (30 minutes)

Leader
Select a member of the group ahead of time to read aloud the Scripture passage. Then discuss the Questions for Interaction, dividing into subgroups of three to six

Paul continues to show how Christ's death brings justification and salvation. Even as death came through Adam, now life and victory over sin comes through Christ. Read Romans 5:12–21 and note how Jesus changes all darkness and death to light and life.

A Comparison Between Adam and Christ

[12]Therefore, just as sin entered the world through one man, and death through sin, in this way death spread to all men, because all sinned. [13]In fact, sin was in the world before the law, but sin is not charged to one's account when there is no law. [14]Nevertheless, death reigned from Adam to Moses, even over those who did not sin in the likeness of Adam's transgression. He is a prototype of the Coming One.

[15]But the gift is not like the trespass. For if by the one man's trespass the many died, how much more have the grace of God and the gift overflowed to the many by the grace of the one man, Jesus Christ. [16]And the gift is not like the one man's sin, because from one sin came the judgment, resulting in condemnation, but from many trespasses came the gift, resulting in justification. [17]Since by the one man's trespass, death reigned through that one man, how much more will those who receive the overflow of grace and the gift of righteousness reign in life through the one man, Jesus Christ.

[18]So then, as through one trespass there is condemnation for everyone, so also through one righteous act there is life-giving justification for everyone. [19]For just as through one man's disobedience the many were made sinners, so also through the one man's obedience the many will be made righteous. [20]The law came along to multiply the trespass. But where sin multiplied, grace multiplied even more, [21]so that, just as sin reigned in death, so also grace will reign through righteousness, resulting in eternal life through Jesus Christ our Lord.

Romans 5:12–21

Questions for Interaction

Leader
Refer to the Summary and Study Notes at the end of this session as needed. If 30 minutes is not enough time to answer all of the questions in this section, conclude the Bible Study by answering question 7.

1. What was the last funeral you attended? How did it make you feel?

2. How do some of your nonbelieving friends or relatives feel about dying and what happens after death? How does that differ from your thoughts?

3. Describe in medical terms how the sin of Adam has affected his descendants to the present day.

   ○ A disease.
   ○ An epidemic.
   ○ A cancer.
   ○ An infection that attacks the immune system.
   ○ Other _____.

4. What are the results of Christ's death for the believer?

5. What is the "gift" Paul refers to five times in verses 15–17? What does one need to do to obtain this "gift" according to verse 17?

6. Paul teaches that those who follow Christ move from being a sinner to being declared righteous, from facing eternal death to living an eternal life. Where are you on this journey?

7. How has God multiplied his grace in your life despite your multiple sins? What does that mean to you?

Going Deeper　　If your group has time and/or wants a challenge, go on to this question.

---

8. What is meant by the phrase, "He is a prototype of the Coming One," in verse 14?

Caring Time Apply the Lesson and Pray for One Another (15 minutes)

Come together now in this time of caring, remembering "the gift" that God has provided through his Son, Jesus Christ. Begin by sharing your responses to the following questions. Then share prayer requests and pray for one another.

Leader
Continue to encourage and mentor the person you identified as being a potential leader for a new small group when your group divides. Conclude the group prayer time today by reading Psalm 105:1–4.

1. This past week did you feel like you were influenced more by the legacy of Adam (sin and death) or the legacy of Christ (holiness and life)? Why?

2. If you were to write a thank you note to God thanking him for "the gift" he gave you, what would you say?

3. How do you need God's help this week in becoming more like Christ?

NEXT WEEK *Today we compared how sin entered the world through Adam, with devastating consequences, to how salvation entered the world through Jesus Christ, with life-giving consequences. We were reminded once again of "the gift" that God gives each of us when we believe in and accept his saving grace. In the coming week, share with someone how thankful you are for all God has done for you. Next week we will look at the freedom we have from sin and death, and how God's grace is not a license to sin but an opportunity to love and serve God.*

Notes on Romans 5:12–21

Summary: Having shown that Christ's death declares us righteous and brings salvation, Paul now shows how the act of one man could have such impact. Through Adam and his one deed of disobedience, the whole human race came to know sin and death. In the same way, by one act of obedience Jesus brings righteousness and eternal life to all who so desire it.

5:12 *sin entered ... through one man.* This is a reference to the sin of Adam in the account of creation and the fall of man found in Genesis 3. The actions of Adam and Eve had consequences for all people to come. Through their sin, sin was evident in all who followed. *death through sin.* Death is the consequence of sin (Gen. 2:17), and so all die because Adam sinned. Jewish teaching said that Adam would have been immortal had he not sinned.

5:14 *death.* More than the physical cessation of life is in view here, since the contrast is always with eternal life (v. 21). Death is a part of the judgment and condemnation (v. 18)—since all have sinned. It is spiritual death as well as physical death that concerns Paul. *Adam.* In Hebrew, Adam's name means "humankind." He is representative of all humanity. *Adam's transgression.* Adam disobeyed God's clear instructions (Gen. 2:17). *prototype.* Literally, a mark or impression that has been left by something. The word "prototype" came to mean a form, type, figure or foreshadow. Adam and his impact on humanity is a prefigure of Christ who would also impact all people.

5:15 *the gift.* This could mean Christ and his work on behalf of humanity, but in light of verses 18, 20 and 21 it probably refers to the status conferred on humanity of being counted righteous before God. Christ's good gift to humanity vastly exceeds in effectiveness the evil legacy of Adam. The contrast is not between one man and many, but between Christ and Adam on the one hand, and the many (i.e., the rest of humankind) on the other.

5:17 *reign in life.* Once death reigned over humans as a tyrant; now it is not that a different ruler has been put in death's place (e.g., "life"), but rather that now believers reign in life.

5:18 *one righteous act.* This indicates that not just his sacrificial death is in view here, but his whole life of obedience. *everyone.* Paul is obviously not using this word in a totally inclusive way, meaning "every single individual." Those who are now believers are not condemned any longer, as he has stated over and over; so condemnation for all people is not an absolute declaration. Likewise, the phrase "life-giving justification for everyone" is also not absolutely inclusive. In Romans 1:16–17 and 3:21–25, Paul makes it quite clear that justification comes to "everyone who believes." Justification is open to all, but it must be accepted by faith.

5:20 *law.* When the Law came, it served to define what was in fact "sinful"—it brought "sin" into the light of day by naming it. *multiply.* Sin increases in the sense that it is now visible and evident. Also, once sin is defined, to continue in it is even worse—it is now willful disobedience. Paul may also mean that the prohibitions actually stimulate more active law-breaking on the part of those who delight in defying God.

Freedom From Sin

Scripture Romans 6:1–2,6–12,15–18,22–23; 7:4–6

> **LAST WEEK** *In last week's session, we considered how one sin by Adam brought death to all humanity; and how one act of righteousness by Jesus brought eternal life to all who accept "the gift." Today we will look at the freedom Christ gives us from the power of sin in our lives, so that we are no longer slaves to sin but free to love and serve God.*

 Ice-Breaker Connect With Your Group (15 minutes)

Leader
Choose one, two or all three Ice-Breaker questions, depending on your group's needs.

The concept of freedom is one that we cherish. In today's passage, Paul talks about freedom from sin and death. Take turns sharing what freedom has meant in your life.

1. What did you most appreciate about your freedom when you first moved away from home?

2. What freedom in the United States would you most miss if it were taken away?

    ○ Freedom of worship.
    ○ Freedom of speech.
    ○ Freedom for both men and women to get an education.
    ○ Freedom to vote.
    ○ Other _____.

3. We all have a bad habit that is a constant struggle. What is the one bad habit that has control of you?

Bible Study Read Scripture and Discuss (30 minutes)

Sin can be extremely defeating. It can demoralize a person to the point that they give up. Paul's letter emphasizes how grace has the power to free people from the defeat sin can bring. The law has no power either. No longer does the believer live by a list of rules and regulations but by the leading of the Holy Spirit. Read the selected parts of Romans 6:1—7:6 and note what true freedom means.

Leader
Select three members of the group ahead of time to read aloud the selected portions of the Scripture passage. Have one member read 6:1–12; another read 6:15–18, 22–23; and the third person read 7:4–6. Then discuss the Questions for Interaction, dividing into subgroups of three to six.

Freedom From Sin

Reader 1:   6 What should we say then? Should we continue in sin in order that grace may multiply? ^{2}Absolutely not! How can we who died to sin still live in it? ... ^{6}For we know that our old self was crucified with Him in order that sin's dominion over the body may be abolished, so that we may no longer be enslaved to sin, ^{7}since a person who has died is freed from sin's claims. ^{8}Now if we died with Christ, we believe that we will also live with Him, ^{9}because we know that Christ, having been raised from the dead, no longer dies. Death no longer rules over Him. ^{10}For in that He died, He died to sin once for all; but in that He lives, He lives to God. ^{11}So, you too consider yourselves dead to sin, but alive to God in Christ Jesus. ^{12}Therefore do not let sin reign in your mortal body, so that you obey its desires. ...

Reader 2: ^{15}What then? Should we sin because we are not under law but under grace? Absolutely not! ^{16}Do you not know that if you offer yourselves to someone as obedient slaves, you are slaves of that one you obey—either of sin leading to death or of obedience leading to righteousness? ^{17}But thank God that, although you used to be slaves of sin, you obeyed from the heart that pattern of teaching you were entrusted to, ^{18}and having been liberated from sin, you became enslaved to righteousness. ... ^{22}But now, since you have been liberated from sin and become enslaved to God, you have your fruit, which results in sanctification—and the end is eternal life! ^{23}For the wages of sin is death, but the gift of God is eternal life in Christ Jesus our Lord.

Reader 3:   7 ^{4}Therefore, my brothers, you also were put to death in relation to the law through the crucified body of the Messiah, so that you may belong to another—to Him who was raised from the dead—that we may bear fruit for God. ^{5}For when we were in the flesh, the sinful passions operated through the law in every part of us and bore fruit for death. ^{6}But now we have been released from the law, since we have died to what held us, so that we may serve in the new way of the Spirit and not in the old letter of the law.

Romans 6:1–2,6–12,15–18,22–23; 7:4–6

Questions for Interaction

Leader
Refer to the Summary and Study Notes at the end of this session as needed. If 30 minutes is not enough time to answer all of the questions in this section, conclude the Bible Study by answering questions 6 and 7.

1. What have you felt like a slave to this past week?

   ○ Work.
   ○ My lifestyle.
   ○ Debt.
   ○ Sin.
   ○ God.
   ○ My house.
   ○ Other _____.

2. In what ways do people become "slaves of sin" (6:17)? What is the result of this slavery? What is the benefit of being "enslaved to righteousness" (6:18)?

3. How does one break free from the bondage of sin?

4. What does Paul mean when he says you have "been released from the law" (7:6)? What are the implications of this for the Christian life?

5. What kind of legalisms do Christians get caught up in? What motivates you to live a good life?

6. In what area of your life do you need to be dead to sin and alive to God?

7. How can you serve in the "new way of the Spirit" (7:6) in the coming week?

Going Deeper If your group has time and/or wants a challenge, go on to this question.

8. Why do you think some Christians view this freedom from "the law" and the abundance of grace as a license to indulge in sin? What does that say about that person's view of grace?

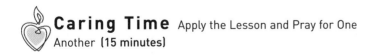 **Caring Time** Apply the Lesson and Pray for One Another (15 minutes)

Leader
Conclude the prayer time today by asking God for guidance in determining the future mission and outreach of this group.

Come together now "in the new way of the Spirit" and encourage one another to die to sin and live for Christ. Begin by sharing your responses to the following questions. Then share prayer requests and close in prayer.

1. On a scale of 1 (not very) to 10 (very), how wholeheartedly did you serve God this past week?

2. How has this group been a help or encouragement to you in your spiritual life?

3. What do you need to do this week to reclaim your freedom in Christ and break free from bondage to sin?

> **NEXT WEEK** *Today we looked at the freedom Christ gives us from the power of sin in our lives. That freedom empowers us to serve God "in the new way of the Spirit" (7:6). In the coming week, commit to being a willing servant of God and see how the Holy Spirit leads you. Next week we will look at how the law of God exposes our struggles with sin.*

Notes on Romans 6:1–7:6

Summary: Paul begins by responding to a potential problem created by his teaching on justification by faith. If what a person does has no merit in terms of salvation and if a believer is already assured of a positive verdict on the Day of Judgment, then why not "live it up" and sin with gusto and impurity because one is already in the kingdom? This was not merely a hypothetical concern. It was happening in the church as is seen in 1 Corinthians 5 and elsewhere. In response to such a misunderstanding, Paul states that justification does have moral implications. Right standing before God yields righteousness of life, and to pretend otherwise is both absurd and profane.

6:1–2 Paul's "opponent" appears once more, questioning Paul in the typical cynical attitude of the day: "If grace is the most wonderful thing there is and if grace multiplies in the presence of sin (5:20), then shouldn't we sin all the more so as to produce yet more grace?" Note that Paul does not deny the doctrine of grace in the face of such a charge. Rather, in verse 2 he first gives a strong negative response to his critic's question and then asks his own question (which points out the absurdity of the position).

6:2 *died to sin.* Paul's point is that his critic's question is logically absurd: to be a Christian is to have died (past tense) to sin; thus it is impossible to live in something one has died to! In verses 3–14, Paul details what it means to have died to sin.

6:6 *old self.* The former unregenerated, preconversion life—what a person once was. ***may be abolished.*** The Greek word means "to be defeated," not "to become extinct." The sinful part of one's nature is not destroyed, but is deprived of power; its domination is broken.

6:7 *freed from sin's claims.* The only way to be freed from sin (literally, "justified from sin") is by paying its penalty. But for the Christian, resurrection follows death, and thus a believer is freed to rise to a new life in which sin cannot dominate.

6:11 *consider yourselves.* To regard, reckon, consider or recognize intellectually that one's old self has died. A Christian's story is told in two parts. Part one, prior to conversion, is now closed. While it is not impossible for a believer to continue to live the same as before conversion, it is incongruous with one's new union with Christ.

6:16 *obey.* In verse 15, the (false) assertion is that since one is not under law any longer (v. 14), one does not have to obey its demands. But Paul points out that everyone obeys one of two masters. To continue sinning is a clear demonstration that sin is indeed master, since sin's demands are obeyed. Rather, under grace a believer is to obey God. Obedience is set in contrast to sin, which is itself disobedience to God. Note that there is no third way. One obeys sin or God. To pretend to have no master is to be in bondage to one's own ego, which in fact is to be a slave to sin.

6:18 *liberated from sin.* Free in the sense of having a new master—God—in place of the old master—sin. Paul is not teaching that Christians do not sin.

6:23 *wages of sin.* Literally, "wages with which to buy food"—a phrase used to describe the rations of cooked meat or fish eaten by soldiers. Roman slaves, too, were given pocket money. *gift of God.* In contrast to the death which sin pays out, God does not pay wages. He is under obligation to no one. Rather, he freely gives eternal life.

7:4 *put to death in relation to the law.* In the same way that death terminates a marriage, a believer's death to sin terminates the condemning power of the Law over that person. *through the crucified body of the Messiah.* When Jesus was put to death on the cross, the death he died was for those who would believe in him. *bear fruit for God.* As a marriage was expected to produce children, so one's new life with Christ is expected to lead to holiness, the result of this union with Christ.

7:5 *sinful passions.* Concrete acts of sin are in view here. *operated through the law.* The prohibitions awaken both the desire to violate them (the fascination of forbidden fruit) and the self-centered impulse to defend oneself from their claim.

7:6 *released from the law.* To the legalist Paul says, "The death of Christ has delivered you from the tyranny of the Law!" *serve.* A Christian is freed from the Law to serve and not to sin—free for obedience, not license. *new way ... old letter.* The Christian serves not the Law in its crippling and binding detail but rather follows the liberating way of the Spirit.

God's Law Reveals Our Sin

Scripture Romans 7:7–13

LAST WEEK *Last week we looked at the freedom Christ gives us from the power of sin and the bondage of the law. We can now live under the control of the Spirit and be free from sin's hold and the burden of legalism. Today we will look at how the Law exposes our sin and the struggle we have with doing the right thing. We will discover that the Law of God is not in the wrong, but it is we who are in the wrong because of our inability to obey God's Law.*

Ice-Breaker Connect With Your Group (15 minutes)

Leader
Choose one, two or all three of the Ice-Breaker questions, depending on your group's needs.

Rules and regulations are a part of our everyday life. We often feel they infringe on our freedom, but in fact they protect us in many ways. Take turns sharing your unique life experiences with following the rules.

1. While growing up, what "law" did your parents have that you dared not break?

   ○ Keeping my room clean.
   ○ Being home by curfew.
   ○ Getting to bed at a certain time.
   ○ Going to church.
   ○ Other _____.

2. What one "law" do you want obeyed in the home you lead?

3. Did you ever get sent to the principal's office while in school? What was the reason?

Bible Study Read Scripture and Discuss (30 minutes)

None of us like getting caught for doing something wrong. And there are not too many of us who like a bunch of rules that we have to abide by. Paul writes here that the rules God gives us (the Law) are not bad. They just expose everyone's wrongdoing. Though we cannot obey God's Law without the help of the Spirit, the Law is still needed to reveal the error of our ways. Read Romans 7:7–13 and note how Paul appreciates what the Law provides.

Leader
Select a member of the group ahead of time to read aloud the Scripture passage. Then discuss the Questions for Interaction, dividing into subgroups of three to six.

God's Law Reveals Our Sin

[7]What should we say then? Is the law sin? Absolutely not! On the contrary, I would not have known sin if it were not for the law. For example, I would not have known what it is to covet if the law had not said, You shall not covet. [8]And sin, seizing an opportunity through the commandment, produced in me coveting of every kind. For apart from the law sin is dead. [9]Once I was alive apart from the law, but when the commandment came, sin sprang to life [10]and I died. The commandment that was meant for life resulted in death for me. [11]For sin, seizing an opportunity through the commandment, deceived me, and through it killed me. [12]So then, the law is holy, and the commandment is holy and just and good.

[13]Therefore, did what is good cause my death? Absolutely not! On the contrary, sin, in order to be recognized as sin, was producing death in me through what is good, so that through the commandment sin might become sinful beyond measure.

Romans 7:7–13

Questions for Interaction

1. Did you ever get in trouble for something at school or home and honestly didn't know it was wrong? What was it? Were you still disciplined for it? If so, how did you feel about that?

2. According to Paul, what purpose does the Law serve?

3. How does sin "seize an opportunity" in our lives "through the commandment" (v. 8)?

Leader
Refer to the Summary and Study Notes at the end of this session as needed. If 30 minutes is not enough time to answer all of the questions in this section, conclude the Bible Study by answering question 7.

4. How does the commandment of God (that was meant for life) result in our death? Why does the Law lack the power to help us overcome sin?

5. How important is reading God's Word to your Christian walk? How do you demonstrate that belief?

6. What commandment of Scripture do you find hard to obey?

   ○ Love your enemy.
   ○ Do not covet.
   ○ Give cheerfully.
   ○ Be submissive.
   ○ Serve one another.
   ○ Other _____.

7. When has sin seized an opportunity in your life and deceived you?

Going Deeper   If your group has time and/or wants a challenge, go on to this question.

8. How do we resolve the apparent conflict on the role of the Law as seen in this passage compared to Paul's previous statements in Romans 5:20 and 6:14?

Caring Time Apply the Lesson and Pray for One Another (15 minutes)

Prayer is a wonderful way to find strength and hope when struggling with sin. Take this time now to share your concerns and pray for one another.

1. What's the immediate forecast for the "weather" in your life?

   ○ Sunny and warm.
   ○ Overcast.
   ○ Chance for showers.
   ○ A big storm is brewing.
   ○ Other _____.

2. What sin are you currently struggling with? How can the group help?

3. What can you give God thanks for despite the struggles you face?

Leader
Following the Caring Time, discuss with your group how they would like to celebrate the last session next week. Also, discuss the possibility of splitting into two groups and continuing with another study (perhaps Book 2 of Romans).

Notes on Romans 7:7-13

Summary: In 7:5 Paul could be understood to be saying that the Law brought to humanity both sin and death. Through two questions put in the mouth of his hypothetical opponent (vv. 7,13) he lays to rest these charges. In verses 7–12 he shows that the Law is not evil (sinful) and in verse 13 he shows that the Law is not that which brings death. Throughout this passage, Paul may be telling of his experience in terms that reflect his solidarity with Adam, as though his experience mirrored that of Adam's. The command in Genesis 2:17 not to eat was given with the good of humanity in mind, but the serpent twisted the benevolent prohibition into a deadly temptation. Prohibition produced covetous desire.

7:7 *Is the law sin?* It might seem that this is what Paul is saying (5:20; 6:14; 7:1–6). In fact, he shows that far from being evil or sinful, the Law serves, first, to reveal sin. It is like a finger pointing, "See that over there, that is what sin is." *I.* In Greek, "ego." Throughout the remainder of chapter 7, Paul uses the first person singular (I, me). In verses 7–13, he is probably using the first person singular in the sense of thinking of himself as a representative of humanity in general. He is not doing this merely for rhetorical reasons, but also because it reflects his own pre-Christian experience. *covet.* Covetousness is an inner attitude in which a person wants what someone else has. People might have never known that covetousness was wrong but for the fact that the Law points it out (Ex. 20:17).

7:8 *opportunity.* This word is used to describe a military base that provides the starting point or bridgehead from which an active assault is launched. *produced in me.* The Law provokes sin (its second function), not simply by pointing out forbidden fruit, but by being misunderstood as setting an unreasonable limitation on one's personal freedom (thus inducing rebellion). *sin.* Paul personifies sin as a vital power with an evil intention. *dead.* Sin is dead in the sense of being "inactive" until a prohibition comes along and rouses it to defiance.

7:9 *alive apart from the law.* Paul may be thinking autobiographically when, as a Jewish child prior to his bar mitzvah at 13, he had no obligation to the Law; or he may be thinking more generally of the period between Adam and Moses (5:13–14).

7:10 *I died.* Though living physically after the Law came, he fell under its judgment; i.e., under the sentence of death. This is the third function of the Law: it identifies the penalty for sin.

7:11 *deceived me.* Compare Genesis 3:13, "The serpent deceived me." The serpent had done so in three ways: First, by distorting God's commandment (Gen. 3:1) in that he ignored the positive ("You are free to eat from any other tree") and focused only on the negative ("but don't eat from this one"). Second, the serpent lied by saying that God would not punish the woman by death (Gen. 3:4). Third, by twisting the commandment itself the serpent cast doubts on God's good intentions and suggested that they should oppose God. This is how sin misuses law.

7:12 *holy.* Literally, "different," i.e., of another realm of existence. The Law is divine both in origin and authority.

7:13 The final question in the series: "Even though it can be shown that the Law is good and not evil, wasn't it the Law that brought death to me? Therefore, isn't the Law bad?" Paul's answer begins with the familiar emphatic denial ("Absolutely not!"). His point is that it is sin that is the culprit, not the Law. In fact, sin reveals its true colors by bringing death through what is good. It is caught red-handed in its distorting work and shown in its utter sinfulness. The Law offered life if it was obeyed, but it lacked the power to enable individuals to overcome sin.

Struggling With Sin

Scripture Romans 7:14–25

LAST WEEK *The purpose of the Law was our topic in last week's session. We saw how the Law exposes our sin and provides a way to know God's will for our lives. We discovered that God's rules and regulations (the Law) are not in the wrong, but that we are in the wrong because of our inability to obey. Today we will conclude this course with a look at our ongoing struggle with sin, which keeps us from obeying God and living in freedom.*

Ice-Breaker Connect With Your Group (15 minutes)

We all have many good goals and objectives we want to accomplish with our lives, but often we let obstacles get in our way. Take turns sharing some of your struggles with accomplishing everything you would like or are expected to do.

Leader
Begin this final session with a word of prayer and thanksgiving for this time together. Choose one or two Ice-Breaker questions to discuss.

1. What New Year's resolution have you started with good intentions only to have it fizzle out?

2. Are you a neat freak or a messy slob? If you had a maid, what would be the first job on your list?

3. If you had to give yourself a grade for obedience as a child, what would it be?

Bible Study Read Scripture and Discuss (30 minutes)

Paul appears to come across as more human here than in any other Scriptures he wrote. We learn that we are not alone in this struggle against sin. Even Paul had his battles. In fact we are quite normal. No wonder we need each other to overcome these struggles. Read Romans 7:14–25 and note how Paul gives thanks despite his frustration.

Leader
Select a member of the group ahead of time to read aloud the Scripture passage. Then discuss the Questions for Interaction, dividing into subgroups of three to six.

Struggling With Sin

[14]For we know that the law is spiritual; but I am made out of flesh, sold into sin's power. [15]For I do not understand what I am doing, because I do not practice what I want to do, but I do what I hate. [16]And if I do what I do not want to do, I agree with the law that it is good. [17]So now I am no longer the one doing it, but it is sin living in me. [18]For I know that nothing good lives in me, that is, in my flesh. For the desire to do what is good is with me, but there is no ability to do it. [19]For I do not do the good that I want to do, but I practice the evil that I do not want to do. [20]Now if I do what I do not want, I am no longer the one doing it, but it is the sin that lives in me. [21]So I discover this principle: when I want to do good, evil is with me. [22]For in my inner self I joyfully agree with God's law. [23]But I see a different law in the parts of my body, waging war against the law of my mind and taking me prisoner to the law of sin in the parts of my body. [24]What a wretched man I am! Who will rescue me from this body of death? [25]I thank God through Jesus Christ our Lord! So then, with my mind I myself am a slave to the law of God, but with my flesh, to the law of sin.

Romans 7:14–25

Questions for Interaction

1. What do you do when you get frustrated with your Christian walk?

   ○ I spend extra time in prayer.
   ○ I talk with other Christians and see how they are doing.
   ○ I tend to go to church less and try to avoid other Christians.
   ○ I try to figure out why I'm having these feelings, so I read and study.
   ○ Other _____.

Leader
Refer to the Summary and Study Notes at the end of this session as needed. If 30 minutes is not enough time to answer all of the questions in this section, conclude the Bible Study by answering question 7.

2. What is your impression of Paul after reading this? Knowing that he wrote most of the books in the New Testament, how does that encourage you?

3. When Paul says that the "law is spiritual" in verse 14, what do you think he means?

4. What is at the root of this battle between our desire to live right and our inability to live right?

5. In the midst of this frustrating struggle, what is Paul's hope?

6. How would you compare your struggle with the power of sin to Paul's struggle?

7. In what area of your life is your spirit willing but your flesh is weak?

    ○ Diet.
    ○ Work habits.
    ○ Spiritual disciplines.
    ○ Exercise.
    ○ Other _____.

Going Deeper   If your group has time and/or wants a challenge, go on to this question.

8. How does Christ rescue us from the "body of death" (v. 24)? What is our part in that rescue?

Caring Time Apply the Lesson and Pray for One Another (15 minutes)

Gather around each other now in this final time of sharing and prayer and encourage one another to persevere in the faith. With Paul, let us "thank God through Jesus Christ our Lord" (v. 25) for our many blessings.

1. What do you need Jesus to rescue you from in the coming weeks?

2. How will you go about doing what is "good" in the area you mentioned in question 7?

3. What will you remember most about this group? How would you like the group to continue to pray for you?

Leader
Conclude this final Caring Time by praying for each group member and asking for God's blessing in any plans to start a new group and/or continue to study together.

WHAT'S NEXT? *Today we concluded this course on Romans, chapters 1–7, with at look at our ongoing struggle with sin. This battle with sin keeps us from obeying God and living in freedom. But, thanks be to God, Jesus Christ is our rescue. To conquer sin we must yield to the rescue and seek encouragement from our Christian community. If your group has decided to continue with studying Book 2 of Romans, the next session will focus on how we are able to overcome this struggle with sin by living in the power of the Spirit.*

Summary: In this section (as in vv. 7–13), the problem is not with the Law but with the sin that dwells within. The Law is good. People want to follow it, but find they cannot—at least not in their own strength. And so tension results. Paul illustrates this conflict vividly out of his own pre-Christian experience. As a sincere and dedicated Pharisee truly seeking God's way, he finds that despite his love of the Law and desire to do good, he cannot escape the domination of sin. (It must be noted that while people like Origen, Wesley and Dodd favor this interpretation of the passage, still others like Calvin, Luther and Barth feel that Paul is talking about his experience as a Christian. They argue that only a mature Christian has a sober enough view of himself to utter the cries of despair in verses 18 and 24, while simultaneously delighting in God's Law as in verse 22.)

7:14 *the law is spiritual.* That is, it comes from God and therefore bears his divine authority It is important for Paul to say this lest his first-century Jewish audience misunderstand him to be departing from Old Testament Law.

7:17 Not an excuse but a confession. "I want to do good but can't." The problem is not with the Law, but with sin.

7:18 *my flesh.* The idea is not that one part of a person is "sinful" while another part is "spiritual." Rather, this is the whole person seen from one point of view; in this case, in terms of unaided human nature.

7:21 *this principle.* Not the Old Testament Law, but the other law mentioned in verse 23. Paul stands back from the experience itself and defines the nature of the conflict in theological terms.

7:22–23 The law of the mind resides in the inner being. It delights in God's Law in contrast to the law of sin, which is at work in the members and at war against God's Law.

7:23 *law of sin.* This is the power exercised over humans by sin.

7:24 The nearer people come to God, the more aware they are of how short they fall of perfection. This is the cry of anguish of one who longs to be free from slavery to sin and domination by the Law. *Who will rescue me.* Since the problem of humanity is indwelling sin, and attempts to obey the Law on one's own power only accent the depth of that sin, people are helpless to deliver themselves. They need someone else to rescue them. This is precisely what God has done through Christ (v. 25).

7:25 Who indeed will rescue him? None other than the Lord Jesus Christ who met Paul on the Damascus Road, through whose death he at last found the long sought-after freedom from slavery to sin and bondage to the Law.

Personal Notes

Personal Notes

Personal Notes

Personal Notes

_____

_____

_____

_____

_____

_____

_____

_____

_____

_____

_____

Personal Notes

Personal Notes

Personal Notes

Personal Notes

Personal Notes

Personal Notes

Personal Notes

Personal Notes

_____

_____

_____

_____

_____

_____

_____

_____

_____

_____